The Complete Roadmap to
HEALING ANXIOUS ATTACHMENT

A 21-Day Path to Break Free from Fear of Abandonment, Calm Obsessive Thoughts, and Feel Safe in Love

Eleanor Mercer

TABLE OF CONTENTS

Rewiring Your Mind for Love: Overcoming Overthinking and Abandonment Fears 4

Understanding Anxious Attachment 10

Breaking It Down 34

Breaking the Cycle of Relationship Anxiety ...54

Overcoming Fear of Abandonment and Rejection 73

Communicating Effectively in Relationships .90

Healing Through Self-Love and Inner Work. 111

Building Secure and Lasting Relationships.. 133

Conclusion: Your New Chapter Begins 155

21 Day Action Plan....................................... 163

References 170

Rewiring Your Mind for Love:
OVERCOMING OVERTHINKING AND ABANDONMENT FEARS

The curious paradox is that when I accept myself just as I am, then I can change.

—Carl Rogers

Have you ever felt like you were "too much" for someone but somehow never enough? No matter how much you gave, it still didn't feel secure. Could love slip away at any moment?

You're not broken if you've ever lived in that tension, always scanning for signs someone might pull away or stop caring. You might simply be experiencing anxious attachment, and you are far from alone.

Nearly half the population has some form of insecure attachment (Levy et al., 2011b). That means millions of people—maybe even people close to you—are carrying invisible patterns that shape how they connect, how they fear, and how they love. And if you're reading this book, chances are, you're someone who feels deeply, loves hard, and wrestles with the anxiety of "what if they leave?"

Let's take a look at someone like Emily.

Emily is the kind of person who pours herself into relationships. She gives and gives—hoping to feel secure and be enough. But when her partner pulls away even slightly—maybe because of a late work meeting or a quiet day—Emily's mind goes into overdrive. *Did I do something wrong? Are they upset? Are they losing interest?*

That flood of fear leads her to seek reassurance: texts, calls, questions. But instead of bringing them closer, the constant need for validation creates distance. And just like that, the cycle repeats.

Maybe you've been there too.

Maybe you've questioned yourself after a short reply, replayed conversations in your head, or felt like love was always just out of reach. If so, you're not "clingy." You're not "needy." You're responding the best way you know how—with a nervous system wired to seek safety in connection.

The good news? These patterns can change.

Understanding Where This All Comes From

Our attachment patterns often begin in childhood—long before we have the words to explain them. If love felt inconsistent, conditional, or emotionally unavailable, your nervous system may have learned that love can't be trusted to stay. That fear follows you into adult relationships.

As researchers Ein-Dor and Hirschberger (2016) explain, anxious attachment is marked by hypervigilance in relationships, a tendency to overanalyze social cues, and deep sensitivity to potential rejection. You might know intellectually that everything is fine, but your body and brain are scanning for danger—just in case. It's exhausting.

But here's the truth: *These patterns were learned. And what was learned can be unlearned.*

My Story

I didn't always know I had anxious attachment. Like many people, I thought I was "too emotional" or that something about me made relationships hard. I found myself stuck in cycles of overthinking, emotional burnout, and confusion—especially when a partner pulled away, asked for space, or didn't communicate the way I needed.

I tried harder. I gave more. I read the texts again and again.

And then, one day, I stumbled across the concept of attachment styles. As I read about anxious attachment, I felt seen for the first time—not judged, just understood. That was the moment my healing began—not because I had it all figured out, but because I could finally say, *"Oh, that's why I do that."*

Once I had language for my patterns, I could start working with them, not against them. And now, I want to help you do the same.

What This Book Will Help You Do

This book is your companion on the path to healing anxious attachment. It's designed to help you understand your emotional responses, quiet the overthinking, and build safe, steady, and real relationships.

You'll learn how to

- recognize and interrupt your attachment triggers.
- shift your inner dialogue from fear to compassion.
- communicate your needs without shame.
- develop secure habits in your everyday relationships.
- reclaim your worth—without outsourcing it to others.

We'll walk through psychology-backed tools, relatable stories, practical exercises, and small but powerful changes you can start making now.

This isn't about changing *who you are*—it's about understanding your story, learning new ways to cope, and reconnecting with the parts of yourself that long for love and belonging.

This Journey Starts with You

This book will compassionately and step-by-step walk you through the layers of your attachment style. It will provide you with tools grounded in psychology and neuroscience to help you respond to your fears differently, shift old beliefs, and create new emotional habits.

You'll discover

- how to self-soothe when your anxiety flares.
- how to stop assuming rejection and start asking for clarity.
- how to break the cycle of overgiving and under-receiving.
- how to build secure relationships without losing yourself.

And yes, you'll also explore how to rewire the beliefs that tell you:

- *"I have to earn love."*
- *"If they need space, I've done something wrong."*
- *"I must be too much."*

Spoiler alert: You're not too much. You never were.

You Don't Have to Do This Alone
Healing is deeply personal, but it doesn't have to be lonely. You'll find real-life stories, reflection prompts, and encouragement throughout this book. You'll learn not just from me but from yourself—because the more you know your patterns, the more power you have to shift them.

There may be moments where it feels uncomfortable. That's okay. Growth always is.

But there will also be moments of freedom—when you finally say what you need, breathe without feeling anxious, or, better yet, stop chasing people who can't meet you halfway.

The Invitation

So here's my invitation to you:

Start this journey with compassion. Not for the person you think you *should* be—but for the person you already are.

The one who loves deeply.

The one who cares too much.

The one who is learning to stay.

The one who is ready to be held, not just hold.

This is the beginning of a different kind of love story that starts with you.

Take your time. Be kind to yourself. And know this above all else:

You are worthy of love that stays.

Let's begin.

Chapter 1:
UNDERSTANDING ANXIOUS ATTACHMENT
Why Do I Feel This Way?

Attachment is not what you do.
It's who you are.

—John Bowlby

The Hidden Force Behind Your Anxiety

Do you sometimes ask yourself, *Why do I get so anxious when someone doesn't text me back?* Or, *Why does a slight disagreement feel like a signal that my partner might leave me for good?*

If you have ever felt that gut-wrenching anxiety over a delayed response or fear from a conflict, you are not alone. These feelings are more than just a reaction to a specific situation—they may result from something more rooted—our attachment style. To move forward from a toxic and hindering attachment style, one must take the first step in understanding the *why* of one's emotions.

It is no secret that, while common, having an anxious attachment style can be disruptive to relationships and significantly impact how you interact with those around you. Attachment Theory, developed by John Bowlby and expanded on by Mary Ainsworth, offers insight into the deep emotional patterns that influence our connections to others (Ainsworth et al., 1978). These patterns often begin to develop when we are born, demonstrating that if, from a young age, there are experiences of inconsistency or neglect, as an adult, this individual will struggle emotionally in their adult relationships.

The Science Behind Attachment

When it comes to understanding where these feelings stem from, we need to have a basic foundation of the science behind our attachments. The Attachment Theory, developed by Bowlby (Holmes, 2014), explains how our early and formative relationships—particularly those with caregivers—shape our ability to connect with others throughout our lives. Bowlby's research revealed that the bonds formed early in one's childhood influence how we interact in relationships as adults, from friendships to romantic ones (Bretherton, 1992).

The main idea when it comes to the attachment theory is that we are wired for connection. We are social creatures, and we need care and connection from the moment we are born to survive. How our caregivers respond to our needs—whether consistently or inconsistently—sets the foundation for how we will feel and act in future relationships.

Based on the way a caregiver responds to a child's emotional needs, attachment theory identifies four primary attachment styles (Benoit, 2004):

Secure

People with secure attachment styles are comfortable giving and receiving love. They trust their partners, feel confident in their worth, and are able to maintain healthy, balanced relationships. Secure individuals tend to feel comfortable with intimacy and independence, knowing how to navigate both. This attachment style has been linked to positive relationship outcomes, including greater relationship satisfaction and emotional regulation (Mikulincer & Shaver, 2016).

Anxious

Someone who experiences anxious attachment styles craves closeness and intimacy but has a deep fear of abandonment. They often feel uncertain about their relationships, constantly worrying whether their partner truly cares about them. This attachment style is characterized by a high need for reassurance and validation from others. These individuals may experience intense emotional highs when they feel loved and significant lows when they perceive any threat to the relationship (Simpson & Rholes, 2017).

Avoidant

People with an avoidant attachment style prefer independence and often struggle with emotional intimacy. They may feel overwhelmed by closeness and tend to distance themselves when their partner seeks more emotional connection. Avoidant individuals may value personal space and autonomy over deep emotional intimacy. Research shows that avoidant attachment is linked to difficulties in forming long-term, emotionally fulfilling relationships (Mikulincer & Shaver, 2016).

Disorganized

A person who experiences a disorganized attachment style exhibits a mix of anxious and avoidant traits, often stemming from unresolved trauma or inconsistent caregiving. These individuals may experience confusion and inner conflict in relationships, sometimes acting in ways that seem contradictory, such as seeking closeness but then pushing people away. This attachment style is often seen in individuals who have experienced abuse or severe emotional neglect during childhood (Main & Solomon, 1990)

Attachment Styles Dictate Relationships

If you identify with anxious attachment, you may have grown up in an environment where love and attention were unpredictable. Perhaps your caregiver was sometimes affectionate and attuned but at other times distracted, emotionally unavailable, or overwhelmed. This inconsistency—being cherished one moment and dismissed the next—can plant deep seeds of insecurity. You may have learned to stay hyper-aware of your caregiver's mood, trying to be "good," "pleasing," or "extra lovable" to keep their attention.

According to Bowlby (1969), the attachment system is biologically driven; children are hardwired to seek proximity to their caregiver for safety and survival. When that proximity feels unstable, it creates internal anxiety. The "Strange Situation" study (Ainsworth et al., 1978) revealed that children with anxious attachment protested separation intensely and struggled to self-soothe when their caregiver returned—highlighting a fear that love could disappear at any moment.

As adults, those with anxious attachment often carry these early emotional blueprints into romantic relationships. While there is a deep yearning for closeness, it is usually accompanied by an intense fear of abandonment. You might constantly worry about whether your partner truly loves you, overanalyze their tone or text messages, or need frequent reassurance to feel safe. Even when things are going well, there's a lurking sense that the connection could slip away.

Psychologists Mikulincer & Shaver (2007) describe this pattern as involving "hyperactivating strategies"—efforts to heighten closeness, gain approval, or avoid rejection. These behaviors are not manipulative—they're protective. They're rooted in the nervous system's learned response to unpredictable love: *"If I can just stay close enough, I'll be safe."*

Understanding where anxious attachment comes from isn't about blame. It's about compassion. Once you recognize that these patterns were born out of a longing for safety and connection, you can begin to meet your emotional needs with kindness rather than self-criticism. Healing begins not with fixing yourself but with *understanding yourself*—and creating new, secure ways of relating to yourself and others.

Signs of Anxious Attachment

When you struggle with anxious attachment, relationships can feel like an emotional minefield. There is an intense fear that you might lose the person you love, but also that the behaviors that come with this attachment style will push the person away.

Recognizing the signs of anxious attachment will help you develop self-awareness of when you are acting and feeling out of fear and doubt rather than from a place of security and confidence.

Emotional Highs and Lows

When you have an anxious attachment style, you often experience intense emotional fluctuations that can feel overwhelming. When they feel securely connected to their partner, they may experience deep joy and a sense of emotional fulfillment. However, even minor shifts in communication or behavior—such as a delayed text response or a change in tone—can trigger feelings of insecurity, self-doubt, or even panic.

This heightened sensitivity to perceived distance, whether real or imagined, can lead to a cycle of anxiety and over-analysis, making relationships feel unpredictable and emotionally exhausting.

Fear of Abandonment and Rejection

One of the underlying fears of someone who struggles with anxious attachment is abandonment. This fear can manifest as excessive worrying about one's partner's commitment to them and the relationship (Lebow, 2022). They may constantly seek reassurance or feel as though they are going to be abandoned or broken up with. The anxiety can lead to behaviors like excessive texting, keeping tabs on their social media activity, or trying to find clues on their genuine feeling, as well as interpreting neutral actions as signs of rejection or disdain.

Overthinking and Needing Constant Reassurance

When our attachment system is activated—when you're unsure if you are emotionally safe in a relationship—your mind often shifts into hypervigilance. Small, everyday moments can suddenly feel loaded with meaning: a short or delayed text response, a distracted look, a change in tone.

These seemingly minor things can trigger a cascade of worry: *Did I do something wrong? Are they upset with me? Are they pulling away?* The anxious mind fills in the blanks, usually with worst-case scenarios.

This is not just "overreacting." It's a learned protective response. When love has felt inconsistent or unpredictable in the past, your brain has likely adapted to expect—and scan for—potential signs of disconnection. According to Mikulincer & Shaver

(2007), this hyperactivation of the attachment system is common among anxiously attached individuals. It's the mind's way of trying to preempt abandonment by staying one step ahead of it, even if that means sacrificing inner peace.

But here's where things can become even more challenging: the more we overthink and seek reassurance, the more pressure our partner may feel. In a secure and understanding relationship, reassurance can be soothing. But when it becomes constant, partners—especially those with more avoidant tendencies—can feel overwhelmed, confused, or even pushed away. This can then confirm the anxious person's worst fears: *I'm too much. They're pulling back. I knew it.* And the cycle repeats.

This is where awareness becomes transformational.

Pause, Breathe, Reflect

One of the first steps to breaking this cycle is recognition. It's when we can catch ourselves in the act of spiraling or seeking reassurance that gives us a powerful moment of choice. Rather than reacting impulsively to a fear-based thought, you can pause and ground yourself. You can ask: *Is this thought a fact, or is it a fear?* You can remind yourself: *My emotions are valid, but they don't always reflect reality.*

Dr. Kristin Neff, a leading researcher in self-compassion, emphasizes the importance of treating yourself with kindness when you're in distress, not criticism. She writes, *"With self-compassion, we give ourselves the same kindness and care we'd give to a good friend"* (Neff, 2003). This is a critical shift for those with anxious attachment: learning to be a secure base for yourself rather than looking only outward for emotional safety.

When we don't pause, negative thought loops can lead to emotional distress, mental exhaustion, and relational strain. Over time, the persistent sense of insecurity can damage not just relationships but also overall well-being. You may start feeling unworthy, ashamed, or like you're "too needy"—none of which are true, but all of which can feel painfully real.

Ignoring these patterns doesn't make them disappear—it usually makes them stronger. Avoiding your inner experiences or invalidating them can deepen cycles of self-doubt, low self-esteem, and emotional dependency. However, when you turn toward your emotions with curiosity and compassion, you begin to break the spell. You begin to create space between your triggers and your responses. You start to regulate instead of react.

The Cost of Anxious Attachment

It is essential to recognize that anxious attachment doesn't just affect romantic relationships—it can infiltrate nearly every aspect of life, taking a toll on emotional well-being, self-worth, and overall happiness. The constant fear of rejection or abandonment can result in chronic stress, making it difficult to not only be present but to enjoy the relationship and not stress.

Over time, this constant negative pattern can lead to feeling exhausted and continuous self-doubt. If these feelings of self-doubt aren't addressed, they can lead to resentment towards their partner and themselves, as they may feel frustrated with their inner feelings.

When we consider the actual cost of anxious attachment, it isn't just about recognizing the signs and triggers—it's also about taking it to the next level and empowering yourself to break free from these patterns to establish healthier and more secure habits.

The Emotional Toll: Stress, Anxiety and Self-Doubt

Living with the constant fear of being abandoned can take a significant toll on both your body and mind. If you have ever experienced that nagging feeling that your partner might pull away, even when there's no real reason to be worried, you are not alone. Unfortunately, this is a familiar feeling and internal battle for people with an anxious attachment style.

Our brain is always on high alert, looking for signs that our partner might be drifting away or losing interest. Even the slightest changes in how they act—like taking longer to reply to a text—can feel like a big deal. This insignificant act, to them, can set off a chain of worry and overthinking, causing one to spiral into "What if this means they're pulling away?" or "What if I'm not enough?".

This constant state of worry doesn't just affect your emotions—it also impacts your body and mind in other ways (Lebow, 2022). The constant stress of feeling like something's wrong can make it hard to focus on other aspects of our lives, such as work, school, or even hobbies you once enjoyed. Your thoughts become wrapped up in figuring out your relationship, and everything else becomes blurry. It's like trying to concentrate on a book while someone's blasting music in the background—it's just impossible.

Not only does this affect us in our waking state, but it can also impact our sleep. It can become hard to turn off when your mind is just non-stop worrying and playing scenarios that did not happen or are perceived as threatening the relationship. The next day can become challenging when we experience restless nights without enough sleep, feeling energized or focused.

Often, when one experiences anxious attachment, they may not immediately notice or recognize that their emotions are stronger and more intensified than usual. Small things can feel like big problems—if we notice our partner seems distracted or distant, this can trigger intense feelings of hurt or rejection. For the partner, it can always feel like they are riding an emotional rollercoaster, and after a while, it can become emotionally and mentally exhausting. The constant feeling of doubt can also impact and erode one's self-confidence, further fueling the narrative of being powerless and insignificant (Ein-Dor & Hirschberger, 2016).

Relationship Struggles: Clinginess, Jealousy and Dis-Trust

Living with anxious attachment can make any relationship—romantic or not, feel like a constant emotional rollercoaster. The last thing you want to do is allow these feelings of fear, doubt, and insecurity to push their heads through—but the reality is behaviors linked to anxious attachment can have that effect. It is easy to fall into patterns of seeking reassurance, checking in constantly, or feeling the need to be in constant touch. While these innocent actions stem from a place of fear, and you are merely seeking validation and innocent reassurance, the reality is they can make your partner feel overwhelmed.

How can this play out?

Conflict and Misunderstandings

When you're constantly checking in or looking for reassurance, it can create tension with your partner. They might start feeling smothered, leading to arguments or misunderstandings. What feels like a need for closeness to you might come across as pressure to them. Over time, this can lead them to want to pull away, which makes you feel even more anxious.

Signs of conflict or misunderstandings might include:

- You feel like you're always trying to get your partner to reassure you.

- Your partner seems frustrated or distant, even when you're just trying to connect.

- Small acts like a missed text message or silence can be a big deal.

Difficulty With Boundaries

One of the most challenging aspects of anxious attachment is navigating boundaries—both yours and your partner's. People with anxious attachment often have difficulty distinguishing their own emotional needs from the needs of others, which can lead to blurred or weak boundaries. In relationships, this can manifest as a deep fear of being "left out" or "abandoned," making it difficult to respect both your need for space and your partner's need.

What Are Boundaries?

Boundaries are the invisible lines that define where you end and another person begins. They protect your emotional, mental, and physical well-being. Healthy boundaries are vital for maintaining a sense of self and for sustaining a balanced, respectful relationship. But for individuals with anxious attachment, boundaries can feel like barriers to connection rather than safeguards.

When you're anxious, you may fear that taking space for yourself or allowing your partner to do so could lead to disconnection. You might feel that the more you give of yourself or stay available, the more secure the relationship will feel. But in reality, this behavior can lead to emotional exhaustion and strain the relationship, creating tension where trust and mutual respect are needed.

The core issue is that fear of abandonment often overrides the natural need for space. The emotional high of connection can feel so essential that anything that threatens it, such as taking time apart or needing emotional distance, can trigger intense anxiety.

Signs of Difficulty With Boundaries
Recognizing when you're struggling with boundaries is the first step to healing and growing.

Here are some signs and cues that indicate boundary issues in your relationship:

Feeling Uneasy When Your Partner Wants Space

- You may feel discomfort or anxiety when your partner expresses the need to be alone or take time for themselves. This discomfort might manifest as worry, jealousy, or even resentment. You might think: *"Why do they need space? Am I not enough for them?"*

- In these moments, it's important to remind yourself that needing space doesn't mean your partner doesn't love you or that they're pulling away. Healthy relationships require togetherness and independence; personal space helps both partners recharge and maintain their sense of self.

Always Feeling the Need to Be Available

- If you feel that you must always be available for your partner—whether through text, phone calls, or in person—this can be a sign of weak boundaries. You may struggle with the idea of having your own time or space apart from your partner, believing that you'll risk abandonment if you don't stay constantly connected.

- In relationships, it's natural to want to feel needed, but it's also vital to maintain your interests, hobbies, and social life. A healthy relationship is one in which both partners can enjoy their individual lives while being emotionally connected.

Constantly Checking in With Your Partner

- A pattern of needing to check in constantly, whether through texts or calls, can indicate a lack of emotional boundaries. For example, you might repeatedly ask, *"What are you doing right now? Are you okay? Why haven't you texted back yet?"* This behavior can come from the underlying fear that your partner might pull away if you're not in constant contact.

- While staying connected is a normal part of relationships, when the need to check in feels more like a compulsion than a natural desire, it can signal that your anxieties are taking the lead. Recognizing this and learning to trust in your partner's love, even when they need space, is essential for cultivating a secure bond.

Difficulty Saying "No" or Respecting Your Own Needs

- If you struggle to say "no" to your partner, even when their requests make you uncomfortable or drain your energy, you may be sacrificing your well-being to avoid conflict or rejection. Similarly, you might feel guilty for expressing your needs, such as the need for alone time or space for your hobbies.

- Healthy relationships are built on mutual respect, including respecting each other's needs and preferences. If you find yourself constantly giving in to your partner's needs at the expense of your own, you may need to revisit the concept of boundaries and understand that it's okay to prioritize your emotional health.

Overcompensating for Your Partner's Needs

- If you often go above and beyond to meet your partner's needs—even when it's at the cost of your own happiness or comfort—you may be enacting a boundary violation. This could mean sacrificing your time, comfort, or self-care to make sure your partner is happy to avoid the fear of losing them.

- It's important to remember that while being supportive is a key part of any relationship, it should be a two-way street. When one partner consistently overextends themselves for the other, it can lead to burnout, resentment, and imbalance.

Feeling Anxious When Your Partner Takes Emotional Distance

- If you feel heightened anxiety when your partner pulls away emotionally, this might point to difficulties with recognizing healthy emotional boundaries. Instead of seeing this space as an opportunity to reflect, relax, or take care of yourself, you might interpret it as a sign that they're losing interest or preparing to abandon you.

- It's crucial to understand that emotional distance does not equate to rejection. People process emotions differently, and some individuals need space to recalibrate. When you respect this, you give your partner the space they need to return with greater emotional clarity—and you give yourself the space to reconnect with your own self-worth.

Why Setting Boundaries Matters

Recognizing these boundary-related behaviors is the first step to creating healthier, more balanced relationships. Setting boundaries is not about pushing your partner away but rather about cultivating the emotional space to grow as individuals. It's about respecting your own needs and your partner's so that both people feel safe, valued, and free to be themselves.

When you begin to respect boundaries—both your own and your partner's—you create a relationship dynamic based on mutual trust and emotional safety. Your relationship no longer hinges on constantly managing your anxieties or fear of abandonment. Instead, it thrives on the understanding that you are both whole people, deserving of time and space to be yourselves.

Increased Jealousy and Suspicion
With anxious attachment, it's easy to feel insecure. You might get jealous or suspicious when your partner talks to someone else or doesn't respond to a message immediately. These feelings, although common, can get out of hand and create unnecessary drama in the relationship.

Jealousy can feel and look like:

- You feel uneasy when your partner interacts with people they're close to.

- You ask questions like "Who were you talking to?" or "Why didn't you reply to my message right away?"

- You might feel insecure, like your partner doesn't care about you as much as you care about them.

Fear of Being "Too Much"
One of the most challenging parts of anxious attachment is the fear of being "too much" for your partner. You

might constantly wonder if you're asking for too much attention or if your need for reassurance is becoming a burden. This fear can lead you to hold back from expressing your feelings, creating even more distance between you and your partner.

Being "too much" might feel like:

- You hesitate to share your emotions because you don't want to overwhelm your partner.

- You worry that your need for attention or reassurance is "too demanding."

- You question whether your feelings are valid or if they're just a sign that you're "too needy."

The Cycle of Anxiety

These behaviors can create a negative cycle. You seek reassurance because you're anxious, but your partner feels overwhelmed, so they pull back. This makes you more anxious, which leads to even more reassurance-seeking. And the cycle continues, making it harder to break the cycle and feel secure in the relationship.

The vicious cycle of anxiety looks like this:

- The more you try to reassure yourself, the more your partner seems distant.

- The more your partner pulls back, the more you feel like you're losing them.

- The tension feels like it's always there, and you can't seem to break the pattern.

Breaking the Cycle

To move forward, it's essential to recognize these patterns and understand how they affect both you and your partner. Here are a few tips to help you break the cycle and build a healthier relationship:

- **Build self-confidence:** Work on feeling secure in yourself and trust that your partner loves you. This can help reduce the need for constant reassurance.

- **Respect boundaries:** Understand that both you and your partner need space to grow and recharge. Boundaries are not a sign of rejection— they're essential for both of you to maintain a balanced, healthy relationship.

- **Communicate openly:** Talk to your partner about your fears and needs and listen to theirs. Open communication can help you both understand each other better and find ways to meet each other's needs without feeling overwhelmed.

- **Practice self-soothing:** When you start to feel anxious, try to find ways to calm yourself down without relying on your partner. This could include mindfulness exercises, deep breathing, or journaling to process your emotions.

By working together with your partner and focusing on self-growth, it's possible to break the cycle of anxious attachment and build a healthier, more balanced relationship. It takes time, but creating a deeper, more secure connection with the person you love is worth it.

The Path to Healing Starts With Awareness

Recognizing that anxious attachment plays a role in your relationship struggles is a powerful first step. It is not and will not be easy to admit or accept, but understanding how this pattern has affected your behavior and emotions can be incredibly freeing. Once you have that awareness, you can start to make fundamental changes in how you relate to your partner and how you view yourself.

Change is possible—it starts with the right tools, a willingness to grow, and a commitment to self-awareness. It's not about fixing everything overnight but taking small and intentional steps to rebuild healthier habits and stronger relationships. With time, patience, and effort, you can create a more secure and fulfilling connection with those around you.

Quiz Time—Discover Your Anxious Attachment Level

This quiz is designed to help you understand the severity of your anxious attachment. This quiz serves as a guide and can be completed more than once to see where you are in the moment.

To complete the quiz, please rate each state with the following scale:

1 = Never
2 = Rarely
3 = Sometimes
4 = Often
5 = Always

Emotional Reactivity

1. I feel anxious when my partner doesn't text or call me back quickly.

2. I overanalyze my partner's tone and words, looking for signs they are upset.

3. I feel like I need constant reassurance that my partner loves me.

4. When my partner is distant, I assume I did something wrong.

5. I experience intense emotional ups and downs in my relationships.

Fear of Abandonment

6. I fear my partner will leave me, even when things seem fine.

7. I feel like I care more about the relationship than my partner does.

8. I feel panicked or desperate when I sense my partner pulling away.

9. If my partner spends time away from me, I feel rejected or unwanted.

10. I feel like I need to be around my partner all the time to feel secure.

Behavioral Patterns

11. I check my phone constantly, waiting for my partner to respond.

12. I avoid bringing up issues because I'm scared my partner will leave me.

13. I sometimes "test" my partner's love by making them jealous or withdrawing.

14. I replay past conversations, worrying I said something wrong.

15. I feel the urge to "fix" things immediately when conflict happens.

Self-Worth & Relationship Dependence

16. I feel unlovable or unworthy when my partner is distant.

17. My mood depends on how my partner treats me that day.

18. I feel like I need a relationship to feel whole and secure.

19. I compare myself to my partner's past relationships and worry I don't measure up.

20. I believe my partner will stop loving me if I don't try hard enough.

Analyzing Your Results

Tally up your score.

20-39 (Mild) You experience occasional anxious thoughts but can manage them. You may need some reassurance, but it doesn't overwhelm you.

40-59 (Moderate) Anxious attachment affects your emotional well-being and relationships. You may struggle with insecurity, but awareness can help.

60-79 (Severe) Anxious attachment has a significant impact on your relationships. You may feel dependent on reassurance, fear abandonment, and experience emotional distress.

80-100 (Very Severe) Your attachment anxiety dominates your relationships. Fear of rejection, emotional reactivity, and self-worth issues may make relationships feel exhausting.

Keep reading to learn how to navigate your attachment style and foster the connection you deserve!

Chapter 2:
BREAKING IT DOWN
Understanding the Root Source of Your Attachment Anxiety

Though no one can go back and make a brand-new start, anyone can start from now and make a brand-new ending.

–Carl Bard

Love should feel safe, warm, and secure, but for those who struggle with anxious attachment, love can feel like an emotional rollercoaster. One moment, it is exciting, thrilling, and motivating; the next, it is terrifying and heartbreaking. If you have ever found yourself overanalyzing a partner's text or feeling a deep sense of panic when there is some emotional distance or disconnect, you are not alone.

The truth is—you were not born anxious in love. That fear, that need for constant reassurance, and that feeling of not being enough—it came from somewhere, and for many people, the root of anxious attachment can be traced back to early childhood experiences.

You Weren't Born Anxious in Love—So Where Did It Start?

As children, we learn more than just how to speak, be polite, or tie our shoes; we also learn what love looks like. The way our caregivers treated us, responded to our needs and made us feel whether that was safe or unsafe shaped our understanding of relationships. If love felt unpredictable, inconsistent, or conditional, this planted the seeds of anxious attachment.

Imagine being an innocent child reaching out for comfort only to be met with occasional warmth but typically distance. Through no fault of your own, it could result from your parents being loving but preoccupied, struggling with the demands of everyday life. Or, maybe they were emotionally inconsistent, where, as a child, you never knew if they would shower you with praise and glory or belittle you with words of disdain and frustration. This unpredictability in response and support can be confusing and overwhelming for a child. It is no wonder that as they get older, they seek stability in their relationships—whether romantic or not.

Childhood Experiences and Attachment Wounds

Children who experience unpredictability often develop survival strategies, such as:

- becoming overly attentive to others' moods in order to avoid upsetting or provoking them.

- seeking reassurance to confirm they are still loved and want to be with them.

- feeling anxious when left alone, fearing abandonment, or when they do not respond in a timely manner to their messages, etc.

Unfortunately, these behaviors do not simply disappear with age; they often persist into adulthood and shape how we approach intimacy and connection. As children, we learn not only language, manners, and skills like tying our shoes but also what love looks like. How our caregivers treat us, how they respond to our needs, and how they make us feel safe or unsafe significantly shape our understanding of relationships. If love felt unpredictable, inconsistent, or conditional, it likely planted the seeds of anxious attachment.

There is a misconception that love is physical, but love isn't just about physical presence—it's about emotional connection (Copley, 2024). A parent who provides food and shelter but struggles to engage emotionally can leave a child feeling unseen and unimportant, the same way a parent who doesn't provide food and shelter and struggles to engage emotionally. The results are the same—connection is crucial. What happens? Over time, this can create a deep-seated belief that they must work hard to be noticed or that their emotions are a burden.

A child in this situation may think:

- *If I were more lovable, they would pay attention to me.*

- *I have to be perfect to get their approval.*
- *Love means constantly proving my worth.*

When these emotionally neglected children become adults, they may seek excessive reassurance in relationships, struggle with self-worth, or feel uneasy when things are going well because deep down, they've learned that love isn't always reliable, but it is also unpredictable.

The Pressure to Be Perfect

Some children grow up in environments where love and approval feel conditional. Perhaps a caregiver expected perfection in school, behavior, or achievements. In these homes, mistakes weren't just mistakes—to a child, they felt like threats to the potential love and acceptance they could receive.

As a result, this can lead to:

- ***Perfectionism in relationships:*** They always try to say the "right" thing or be "good enough" to avoid rejection.

- ***Fear of conflict:*** They will avoid difficult conversations out of fear that they will push a partner away.

- ***Difficulty believing in unconditional love:*** They have been conditioned to feel like affection has to be earned rather than freely given or received.

When these childhood patterns are left unaddressed, they shape how we experience adult relationships, creating cycles of insecurity and emotional exhaustion.

How Childhood Attachment Wounds Show Up in Adult Relationships

While it isn't always blatantly obvious, how we experience love in childhood influences how we engage with partners as adults. Some signs of unresolved attachment wounds include:

- **Relationship anxiety:** Constantly worrying that a partner will leave or stop loving you.

- **Overanalyzing everything:** Reading too much into text messages, changes in tone, or minor shifts in typical normal behavior.

- **Fear of rejection:** Feeling panicked when there is emotional distance, assuming it means the relationship is ending.

- **Low self-esteem in love:** Believing you have to earn love by being "perfect."

- **Seeking constant reassurance:** Needing frequent validation to feel secure in a relationship.

These behaviors aren't random—they stem from a deeply ingrained fear that love isn't stable or guaranteed. But the good news is that these patterns can be changed, and the cycle can be broken.

Healing Starts With Awareness

Healing begins when we recognize and understand where our anxiety and attachment fears come from. When we connect the dots between our past experiences and how they show up in our relationships today, we gain the power to break free from old patterns. It's like having a map to understand why we feel the way we do—and with that map, we can choose a different direction.

Here's the thing: your anxious attachment isn't a flaw. It's a learned survival mechanism. It develops in coping with the emotional experiences you had growing up (Copley, 2024). You were doing what you needed to do to feel loved and safe in an unpredictable environment. As adults, these survival strategies are no longer necessary; they hinder us rather than benefit us. It's time to permit yourself to change, to stop reacting out of fear, and to start responding from a place of understanding and growth.

Your anxious attachment is not a flaw. It's a learned survival mechanism. You didn't choose it, but you have the power to heal from it. It helped you get through challenging moments when you were younger, but now, it's time to rewrite that story.

The fears you carry today were once necessary coping strategies. The fear of abandonment, the constant need for reassurance, the overthinking—these were ways you protected yourself as a child when love felt inconsistent or conditional. They helped you survive emotional uncertainty but may be holding you back from the loving relationships you deserve.

You can reshape your experience of love and connection. Once you become aware of the patterns you've been repeating, you can start making small but powerful changes. Healing anxious attachment takes time, but every step forward is a victory. The more you practice awareness and self-compassion, the more you'll shift from fear-driven responses to healthy, secure ways of relating to yourself and others.

Cultivating Healing Awareness in Your Daily Life

You can start creating change today by practicing awareness and making small shifts in your daily habits. Healing doesn't happen overnight, but by implementing simple steps, you can slowly rewire old patterns and create a new, healthier attachment style.

Start with daily reflection. Take a few minutes daily to reflect on your emotional responses, especially when you feel anxious or insecure. Think about moments when you felt triggered—did a text message go unanswered? Did a minor shift in tone leave you feeling uncertain? Reflect on how you responded. Did you feel overwhelmed by fear? Did you seek reassurance? Writing down these thoughts in a journal can be incredibly helpful.

Journaling lets you track patterns, note progress, and see how far you've come. You might even discover triggers that you didn't realize were contributing to your anxiety.

Practice self-compassion. When those feelings of anxiety, self-doubt, or fear of abandonment crop up, remember to be gentle with yourself. It's easy to slip into self-criticism, thinking you're "too needy" or "too much," but those feelings are part of your past, not who you are now. Instead of judging yourself, try practicing self-compassion. When you feel anxious, remind yourself that these feelings are natural, especially when love feels uncertain or unsafe.

Try saying to yourself, *"It's okay to feel this way. I'm doing the best I can and worthy of love, even when I'm anxious."* Think of this as reparenting yourself, offering the same kindness and understanding you would to a friend who is struggling.

Challenge negative beliefs about love. If you've internalized negative beliefs about love, like *"I have to be perfect to be loved"* or *"I'm not worthy of secure love,"* it's important to challenge them. Ask yourself where these beliefs came from. Are they rooted in past experiences, or do they reflect the reality of your current relationships? You may discover that these beliefs are more about your past and less about your present.

The goal is to replace old, limiting beliefs with healthier, more realistic ones. For example, instead of thinking, *"I'll always be abandoned,"* you can remind yourself, *"I am capable of healthy relationships, and I am worthy of love as I am."* Over time, these new beliefs will help you feel more secure and grounded.

Recognize and manage triggers. Healing isn't about avoiding triggers altogether. It's about learning how to manage them when they arise. Pay attention to the moments when you feel your anxiety start to spike—whether it's an unanswered text, a missed call, or a slight shift in your partner's behavior.

These triggers are growth opportunities. Instead of reacting immediately, take a moment to breathe and check in with yourself. Ask, *"What's really going on here? Is this fear or a genuine issue?"* Often, when we pause and reflect, we realize that our anxiety has little to do with the current situation and everything to do with our past experiences.

Seek professional support if needed. Sometimes, the wounds from our past are so deep that healing on our own feels impossible. And that's okay. If you feel stuck in old patterns and need additional support, consider working with a therapist specializing in attachment theory.

A therapist can help you understand your attachment style, process past wounds, and learn how to create healthier relationships. They can also provide the guidance and support you need to overcome any resistance or fear during the healing process.

Healing Takes Time—But It's Worth It

Healing your anxious attachment style is not a quick fix. It's a journey that requires patience, dedication, and, most importantly, self-compassion. Change takes time, and there will be moments where you feel like you've fallen back into old patterns. But that's part of the process. Every step you take toward understanding and healing is closer to the healthy, secure relationships you deserve.

Remember, you are not defined by your attachment style. It doesn't dictate who you are or what you're capable of. Your attachment style is simply a pattern that can be changed. You are not stuck in the past. You can create new experiences, new responses, and new relationships.

So, take the first step. Embrace awareness, practice self-compassion, challenge outdated beliefs, recognize your triggers, and don't be afraid to ask for help if you need it. Healing is possible, and you are more than capable of it. Your journey to a more secure attachment style begins with the simple act of awareness, and from there, the possibilities for love, connection, and happiness are endless.

Relationship Patterns—How Heartbreak Influences the Future

Understanding how our past heartbreaks and emotional trauma influence our relationship patterns is essential in recognizing why certain behaviors feel automatic if not second nature. When you have an anxious attachment style, these patterns often manifest in repetitive cycles, even in new relationships. The previous pain can linger, leaving invisible scars that make it challenging to trust new partners or to open up in healthy ways. Consequently, healing from past trauma is vital not only for our emotional well-being but also for creating a healthier foundation for a future relationship.

Often, we think heartbreak is just romantic—this is not true. Heartbreak can also be experienced with family dynamics. The one thing that heartbreak, regardless of the dynamic, does is leave a mark on our emotional landscape. For the anxious attachment partner, past heartbreak can further reinforce their fear of abandonment. If someone has faced rejection or betrayal in the past, their ability to trust others is deeply affected. The fear of being hurt again can lead to feelings of insecurity, self-doubt, and heightened sensitivity to any signs of emotional distance from a partner.

Heartbreak affects not only our emotional landscape but also dramatically reshapes how we connect in new relationships. Consider someone who has endured a painful breakup; they might step into a new relationship with their defenses raised, traumatized by the possibility of experiencing that same emotional pain again. The unresolved past and wounds of the anxious partner can inadvertently sabotage what could be a beautiful and thriving relationship before it has been given a chance to blossom.

The Cycle of Unavailable Partners

One habit that anxious attachment individuals tend to struggle with is the gravitation towards emotionally unavailable partners, whether consciously or not; however, doing this often results in repeating the unhealthy cycles of attachment. This repetitive pattern is subtle and often unrecognized (McMurtrie, 2022). This may seem counterintuitive, especially if they consciously desire a loving and fulfilling relationship. However, these patterns can feel familiar—dating someone emotionally unavailable might evoke a false sense of security, as it resembles experiences they have always known. In their potential partner, they see in themselves what they lack yet are familiar with.

Relationships that are characterized by emotional distance can intensify feelings of inadequacy, further fueling the cycle of dependency and anxious attachment behaviors. For example, when an anxious partner is with someone who is emotionally distant, the anxious partner will seek and crave affection and attention, which can inadvertently push the partner away. This rejection and emotional distance, unfortunately, just further reinforce the anxious partners' fears of abandonment, resulting in a cycle of desperate attention, validation, and anxiety.

The Self-Sabotaging Nature

The cycle of seeking emotionally unavailable partners and then sabotaging these relationships with anxious behaviors is a form of self-protection (Peel et al., 2019). It's as if the subconscious believes maintaining distance in relationships will prevent future heartbreak. Unfortunately, this strategy often backfires more than not. By pushing away potential partners through insecurity and overdependence, individuals with anxious attachments may unknowingly sabotage their chances of achieving healthy, secure relationships.

The root of this self-sabotage lies in unresolved trauma, whether from childhood or past relationships, which unfortunately keeps individuals trapped in a state of fear and emotional reactivity. To break free from this cycle, it is essential to acknowledge past relationships and use them to recognize that their new or potential partner will not mirror the same past mistakes. For an anxiously attached individual to heal and move forward, it will require that they address the wounds left by previous traumas while also taking the time to emotionally and mentally heal.

Media, Societal and Cultural Implications
While past traumas play a prominent role, societal and cultural pressures and expectations also have a role. The media we consume shapes cultural expectations around relationships; these external factors can reinforce unhealthy attachment styles and contribute to feelings of inadequacy, pressure, and anxiety (Strand et al., 2019). In the age of instant gratification, the impact of societal influences on attachment anxiety has never been more apparent.

Movies, TV shows, and books often portray love as a perfect, effortless experience. Romanticized love stories are filled with grand gestures, dramatic declarations of affection, and unrealistic portrayals of "happily ever after." While these portrayals are entertaining, they set unrealistic expectations for real-world relationships. For someone with anxious attachment, these portrayals can amplify feelings of inadequacy, making them feel like their relationship should look or feel a certain way to be "right."

For instance, the idea that a partner should always "know what you need without asking" or that "true love conquers all" can lead to the belief that if your relationship isn't meeting these idealized expectations, then it's somehow flawed. This can lead to unnecessary anxiety and dissatisfaction as the individual compares their actual relationship to the fictionalized versions they see in the media.

These portrayals can create a sense of urgency around love, making people feel like they need to find "the one" quickly and intensely. Unfortunately, this can only further fuel anxious attachments by creating a sense of dependency and pressure to make a relationship work at all costs, even when it may not be healthy or appropriate for both individuals involved.

Cultural Expectations Around Marriage and Relationships

Beyond media influences, societal and cultural expectations around relationships and marriage can further heighten attachment anxiety. In many cultures, there is tremendous pressure to form a partnership, get married, and live a "happy" life by following traditional milestones. This cultural script often leaves little room for individual differences in relationships that unfold. People with an anxious attachment internalize these expectations, feeling as though they must meet these standards or risk being judged, rejected, or seen as failures.

The pressure to conform to societal norms only adds fire to an anxious attachment's insecurity. When an anxious individual fears falling short of society's expectations, this sense of inadequacy and lack of worthiness can result in a rushed, forced, or false sense of relationship. When this happens, it can actually mask both an individual's values and needs.

Instant Gratification and Dating Apps

Dating is challenging enough—throw in the mix of technology, especially dating apps, and it has added a new layer of complexity to attachment anxiety. The instant gratification model that many apps provide—swiping, matching, and getting quick responses—has created a cycle of validation-seeking. In the case of someone with anxious attachment, the thrill of receiving attention and the anxiety of waiting for responses can trigger emotional highs and lows (Smith, 2024). This constant pinging of validation can reinforce feelings of insecurity and the need for constant reassurance.

The ease of access to potential partners on dating apps can create an environment where it feels like there's always someone better, leading to comparisons and fears of being abandoned or replaced. This can exacerbate anxious attachment patterns, as the validation cycle encourages people to seek constant affirmation from others while also fearing that any emotional misstep might lead to rejection.

While there are benefits to hearing from a potential partner, the reality is that instant gratification, unfortunately, does not allow time for a real connection to form (Molina, 2024). Relationships built on brief exchanges often lack the depth necessary to foster trust and security, leaving anxiously attached individuals feeling unfulfilled or uncertain. This contributes to a vicious cycle of seeking out external validation without fostering internal self-worth.

Understanding the Root of Your Anxiety

Understanding the root causes of attachment anxiety, both from personal experiences and societal influences, is the first step in breaking free from unhealthy patterns. Trauma from past relationships and childhood wounds, combined with cultural and societal pressures, can create a distorted view of love and self-worth. When you can acknowledge these influences, it gives individuals the opportunity to begin the healing process.

To break free from these patterns, it's important to identify unhealthy cycles, challenge societal norms, and work toward building healthier relationship habits. Understanding the role of trauma in attachment and recognizing how external pressures impact personal beliefs can help individuals make conscious choices in their relationships, leading to healthier, more secure connections.

Take Action—Journal Reflection and Self-Reflection Exercises

Here are some journal prompts to encourage self-awareness and reflection on the root source of attachment anxiety:

Exploring Early Influences

- What messages did you receive about love, safety, and relationships as a child?

- How did your primary caregivers respond to your emotional needs? Were they consistent, inconsistent, or absent?

- Can you recall a time in childhood when you felt secure or, conversely, deeply abandoned? How did that experience shape your beliefs about relationships?

Identifying Patterns in Relationships

- Do you tend to feel anxious, fearful, or overly dependent in relationships? When did you first notice this pattern?

- What specific situations in relationships trigger your attachment anxiety? (e.g., not getting a text back, feeling ignored, uncertainty about someone's feelings)

- Have you ever felt like you needed to prove your worth in a relationship? Where do you think that belief comes from?

Unpacking Core Fears

- What are your biggest fears when it comes to love and connection? Do you fear abandonment, rejection, or not being enough?

- How do you react when you start feeling insecure in a relationship? Do you withdraw, seek reassurance, or become overly accommodating?

- If you could speak to the part of yourself that feels anxious in relationships, what would you say to reassure them?

Challenging and Reframing Beliefs

- What are some core beliefs you hold about yourself when it comes to love and attachment? Do you believe you are worthy of love and security?

- Are there times when your attachment anxiety has led you to assume the worst? How often do your fears actually come true?

- What evidence do you have that you can form secure and stable relationships?

Shifting Toward Healing

- What does a secure, loving relationship look like to you? How does it feel?

- How can you begin to self-soothe and provide the reassurance you often seek from others?

- What is one small step you can take today to build a stronger sense of security and self-trust in your relationships?

These prompts guide the reader through a journey of self-discovery, helping them trace the origins of their attachment anxiety and begin shifting their mindset toward healing.

Quiz Time: Recognizing the Cycle of Reassurance-Seeking

This quiz will help you identify your tendencies to seek reassurance in relationships. These behaviors are typical among those with anxious attachment styles. Rate each statement from 1 (never) to 5 (always).

1. I frequently ask my partner or friends if they love or care about me.

2. I sometimes check in with others to ensure they're not upset with me, even if they haven't shown any signs of being upset.

3. When I feel insecure, I often turn to others for affirmation or validation.

4. I feel anxious when I don't receive a prompt response to a message or phone call.

5. I tend to overanalyze conversations or interactions to make sure I haven't said or done something wrong.

6. I feel unsettled or worried when I haven't heard from someone I care about for a while.

7. I ask people close to me frequently if I'm doing things right or if I've upset them.

8. I feel reassured when I receive positive feedback or compliments from others, but the feeling quickly fades.

9. I tend to over-apologize, even when I haven't done anything wrong, just to avoid conflict.

10. I feel a strong need to be reassured that I am loved or accepted by others, especially when I feel anxious.

Analyzing Your Results

10-20: You seek reassurance occasionally, but it doesn't dominate your relationships

21-35: You may seek reassurance frequently, and this can sometimes strain your relationships or increase your anxiety.

36-50: You have a high need for reassurance, and this behavior may lead to cycles of anxiety and emotional instability in relationships.

Chapter 3:
BREAKING THE CYCLE OF RELATIONSHIP ANXIETY

The most important thing in a relationship is not the feeling of love, but the ability to manage the fear of losing it.

–Dr. Harville Hendrix

The Mind as a Barrier to Love

What if your beliefs about love are the very things keeping you stuck? What if the anxiety you experience in relationships isn't a problem with your partner but instead reflects our deep and subconscious fears and patterns?

Relationship anxiety can feel overwhelming, but the good news is that it doesn't have to dominate your life. By understanding the influence of your thoughts, emotions, and self-perception, you can begin to break free from anxious attachment and cultivate healthier, more secure relationships.

Rewiring Negative Thought Patterns

Do you ever find yourself replaying a catchy or annoying song in your mind? It is just on constant repeat? Anxious thoughts play on a loop for someone with an anxious attachment—they replay conversations, think of the worst-case scenarios, and reinforce feelings of insecurity and doubt. When left unchecked and unaddressed, these thoughts can dictate many of our actions, resulting in clinginess, excessive reassurance-seeking, and self-sabotage (Newman et al., 2015).

Anxious thought: "They haven't texted back. They must be pulling away."

Secure thought: "They're probably just busy. It doesn't mean they don't care."

You can train your brain to think more securely.

What's the key to breaking the loop?

Cognitive Behavioral Therapy (CBT)

CBT is one of the most effective therapeutic approaches for managing anxiety, including relationship anxiety (Brandon, 2022). It focuses on identifying and restructuring negative thought patterns that fuel anxious behaviors.

Here's how you can apply CBT techniques to your relationships:

- **Identify the thought:** When you feel anxious about your relationship, pause and ask: What is the exact thought causing this feeling? Example:

"They haven't texted back, so they must be mad at me."

- **Challenge the thought:** Is there actual evidence to support this belief? What are alternative explanations? Example: *"They might just be busy or forgot to respond."*

- **Reframe the thought:** Shift your perspective to a more balanced and realistic one. Example: *"Their delay in texting doesn't define our relationship. I am still loved and valued."*

Recognizing and Reframing Cognitive Distortions

Cognitive distortions are irrational thought patterns that can fuel anxiety and negatively impact relationships. These distortions act as mental filters, shaping how we interpret our partner's actions and words in ways that reinforce our fears. By identifying and addressing these patterns, we can develop healthier and more balanced perspectives in our relationships.

Some common distortions include:

- **Catastrophizing:** Assuming the worst will happen, even when there is little or no evidence to support it. For example, *"They didn't say 'I love you' today. Maybe they're falling out of love with me."* This type of thinking can lead to unnecessary worry and emotional distress. Instead of jumping to conclusions, try reframing the thought: *"They might be stressed or* *distracted. One moment doesn't define our entire relationship."*

- **Mind reading:** Believing you know what someone is thinking without evidence. Example: *"They seem distant; they must be losing interest."* Instead of assuming the worst, ask for clarification: *"You seem quieter than usual. Is everything okay?"*

- **All-or-nothing thinking:** Viewing situations with an extreme perception. For example: *"If they're not constantly affectionate, they must not care at all."* This kind of thinking ignores the natural fluctuations in closeness and expression that occur in healthy relationships.

  A more balanced perspective might be: *"People express love in different ways and at different times. A moment of distance doesn't mean a lack of care."* Recognizing this can help prevent unnecessary anxiety and misinterpretations of your partner's behavior.

- **Personalization:** Assuming that your partner's mood or actions are directly related to something you did, even when there is no clear evidence. This can lead to unnecessary guilt and over-apologizing. Consider, *"They're in a bad mood; I must have upset them."* Rather than thinking this, remind yourself: *"Their emotions are not always about me."*

People have bad days for many reasons that have nothing to do with me." Another example: If your partner seems distracted at dinner, you might assume, *"They must be bored with me,"* when they could be thinking about work stress or personal matters. To combat personalization, practice asking yourself, *"Is there concrete evidence that I caused this? Or could there be another explanation?"* This simple shift in thinking can prevent unnecessary anxiety and improve communication in relationships.

- **Overgeneralization:** When we take one isolated incident or piece of evidence and apply it broadly to every situation. This type of thinking can lead to feelings of insecurity and anxiety in relationships because we assume that one negative event is a sign of a much bigger issue.

  For example, your partner cancels plans with you once, and immediately, you think, *"They canceled our plans once—this means they don't prioritize me."* Instead of recognizing that plans can be canceled due to factors beyond their (or your) control, you start to worry that your partner is no longer interested in the relationship. You might even assume that this means they no longer care about you.

By catching these distortions in action and replacing them with rational, balanced thoughts, you can reduce the intensity of your relationship anxiety.

Practicing Mindfulness to Stay Present

When you experience anxiety in a relationship, it's common for your mind to jump to worst-case scenarios or to overanalyze every interaction excessively. You may constantly worry about your partner's behavior, questioning if they are pulling away. In these moments, practicing mindfulness can help you step back from these anxious thoughts and focus on what is happening right now.

When we pause and practice mindfulness, we are encouraged to be fully present with our partner rather than getting lost in what might go wrong. For example, if your partner seems distant or distracted, instead of assuming they are falling out of love, mindfulness helps you realize that this moment does not define your entire relationship. It allows you to recognize your feelings of anxiety without letting them take control.

Psychological research shows that mindfulness can improve emotional well-being by increasing awareness and reducing reactivity (Keng et al., 2011). In relationships, being mindful means paying attention to your thoughts, emotions, and actions without becoming overwhelmed by them. For individuals who struggle with relationship anxiety, practicing mindfulness can be a valuable tool to promote emotional regulation and foster healthier connections with their partners. By being present, you can respond to your partner more thoughtfully and compassionately, ultimately strengthening your relationship.

Practical Mindfulness Techniques

It is always easier said than done; however, with practice and patience, paired with an awareness of our thoughts and feelings, we achieve a level of control, but more importantly, mindfulness. Practicing mindfulness helps one stay grounded and present rather than thinking of the worst-case scenarios or projecting one's fears and anxieties.

Here are a few mindfulness exercises to help with your anxieties:

- **Mindful breathing**: When you start to feel anxious, take a few deep, slow breaths. Inhale for a count of four, hold for four and exhale for four. This helps calm your nervous system and bring you back to the present moment. For example, if you feel anxious because your partner hasn't responded to a text, pause for a moment and focus on your breath. Instead of jumping to conclusions, use your breath to steady yourself and create space to choose a more balanced response.

- **Observing your thoughts**: Instead of getting lost in your anxious thoughts, observe them. Imagine you're sitting on the edge of a river, watching the thoughts float by like leaves. You don't have to engage with them or judge them; observe. If you're worried your partner isn't texting back because they're mad at you, observe the thought without acting on it. Instead of reacting impulsively, take a step back and allow yourself to recognize that not all thoughts need to be acted upon.

- **Body awareness**: Anxiety often manifests physically in your body—tight shoulders, a racing heart, shallow breathing. By tuning into your body and noticing where you're holding tension, you can begin to release it. A simple exercise is to scan your body from head to toe, noticing any areas of tension. If you notice your shoulders are tight, try to consciously relax them. This body awareness can help reduce the emotional intensity of anxious moments.

- **Mindful listening**: In relationships, anxiety can sometimes make us focus more on what we want to say or on our fears than on genuinely listening to our partner. Practicing mindful listening can help you stay present with your partner's words, tone, and body language. This helps reduce anxiety and fosters a greater understanding and connection. The next time your partner shares something, try to listen without preparing a response in your mind. Just focus on their words and the feeling behind them. This simple act of being present can make a significant difference in reducing anxiety and building intimacy.

- **Grounding exercises**: These exercises help bring you back to the present moment when anxiety or negative thoughts arise. For example, you can use the 5-4-3-2-1 technique, which helps you ground yourself by focusing on your senses. You might say to yourself, "I see the couch, I hear the birds outside, I feel the carpet beneath my feet, I smell the coffee brewing, I taste the mint on my tongue." This technique helps shift your attention away from anxious thoughts and reconnects you to your surroundings.

Nurturing Your Emotional Regulation

Relationships can bring immense joy, but they can also lead to anxiety, especially for those who struggle with emotional regulation. Emotional regulation refers to the process of managing and responding to emotional experiences in a healthy and constructive way. Without these skills, anxiety can overwhelm you, resulting in impulsive reactions that potentially could harm your relationships.

To reduce anxiety and improve emotional well-being, it's important to understand how to regulate your emotions, soothe yourself, and cultivate a sense of self-security. Learning and exploring various techniques for managing anxiety in relationships, such as self-soothing strategies, grounding exercises, and self-validation, can better prepare you for navigating relationships and handling anxiety effectively.

Understanding Emotional Regulation

Emotional regulation is an essential skill that helps us manage our emotional responses in different situations. It means being able to recognize and understand our emotions and then using strategies to respond in a healthy and effective way. For those who experience anxiety, especially in their relationships, emotional regulation can be quite a challenge. Anxiety often leads to intense emotional reactions, resulting in overthinking and impulsive behaviors that can negatively affect the relationship.

Studies have shown that people who struggle with emotional regulation are more likely to face chronic anxiety and stress, particularly in their interactions with others (Gross, 2002). If someone with relationship anxiety feels uncertain or insecure, they might be flooded with fear or doubt. Without the tools to manage those emotions, they may act impulsively—becoming clingy or withdrawing—which can create tension and increase anxiety in the relationship.

The good news is that emotional regulation is something you can learn and improve over time. With practice, you can find healthier ways to manage your emotions, lessen your anxiety, and build more balanced and fulfilling relationships.

Self-Soothing Techniques

One of the most effective ways to manage anxiety is to learn self-soothing techniques. Self-soothing involves calming your mind and body when emotions feel overwhelming. The goal is to reduce emotional reactivity, allowing you to respond to challenging situations in a more balanced and thoughtful way. Below are several self-soothing techniques that can help ease anxiety and bring a sense of peace.

Deep Breathing

Deep breathing is one of the most widely recommended techniques for calming the nervous system. This simple practice involves breathing deeply and slowly, which activates the parasympathetic nervous system—the part of the body that controls relaxation. To practice deep breathing:

1. Inhale deeply through your nose for four seconds.

2. Hold your breath for four seconds.

3. Exhale slowly through your mouth for four seconds.

Repeat this process for several minutes. Research has shown that deep breathing can reduce symptoms of anxiety and stress by slowing the heart rate and lowering blood pressure (Jerath et al., 2015). By practicing deep breathing regularly, you can train your body to respond calmly in moments of anxiety.

Progressive Muscle Relaxation (PMR)

PMR is another powerful self-soothing technique that helps reduce physical tension associated with emotional distress. This technique involves tensing and then releasing different muscle groups throughout the body, starting from your feet and working your way up to your head. This process helps you become more aware of areas where you hold tension and encourages the release of that tension.

To practice PMR:

1. Start by tensing the muscles in your feet for five seconds, then release and relax them for ten seconds.

2. Move to your calves, thighs, abdomen, chest, arms, and face, tensing and relaxing each muscle group.

PMR has been shown to reduce symptoms of anxiety and improve overall emotional well-being (Benson et al., 1975). It can be particularly helpful in moments of heightened stress or anxiety in relationships, allowing you to calm your body and mind.

Grounding Exercises to Detach From Emotional Triggers

When anxiety becomes overwhelming, grounding exercises can help bring you back to the present moment. These techniques focus on using your senses to reconnect with your surroundings, helping to interrupt anxious thought patterns and shift your attention away from distressing emotions.

5-4-3-2-1 Technique

The 5-4-3-2-1 grounding exercise is a simple and effective way to redirect your focus when anxiety takes over. To practice this technique, follow these steps:

- **5 things you see:** Look around and identify five things in your environment.

- **4 things you can touch:** Notice four objects you can physically touch, such as your clothing, the floor, or furniture.

- **3 things you hear:** Pay attention to the sounds around you.

- **2 things you can smell:** Identify two smells, whether from the environment or your own body.

- **1 thing you can taste:** Focus on one taste in your mouth, whether it's the remnants of food or simply the taste of your saliva.

This exercise helps redirect your attention away from anxious thoughts, bringing your focus back to the present moment. According to cognitive behavioral theory, grounding techniques like this can interrupt patterns of rumination and reduce anxiety (Hoffman & Hercus, 2000).

Temperature Change

Another grounding technique involves using temperature to shift your body's focus. You can splash cold water on your face, hold ice cubes in your hands, or step outside into the cold air. The shock of cold can activate the body's calming response, lowering the intensity of emotional arousal. Research has shown that temperature changes can help lower stress and bring a sense of relief in moments of high anxiety (Hoffman & Hercus, 2000).

Cultivating Self-Security

Often, when an anxious person finds a partner, they pour their whole self into that relationship, taking on their hobbies and interests. In essence, they lose their identity; however, one way of managing relationship anxiety is learning to find security within oneself rather than depending on external validation.

Relationship anxiety often stems from a fear of abandonment or a lack of self-worth. When you're constantly seeking reassurance from your partner, you may inadvertently contribute to the anxiety you're trying to avoid. Cultivating a sense of self-security can help you feel more confident and less reliant on your partner for emotional stability.

Learning to Self-Validate

Self-validation involves recognizing and accepting your worth rather than seeking constant reassurance from others. It is an important skill for reducing anxiety in relationships. Don't wait for your partner to affirm your value; try developing your own internal affirmations. Some examples include:

- "I am enough as I am."

- "My worth is not defined by how much attention I receive."

- "I am loved and secure, even when my partner is not immediately available."

When you practice self-validation, you begin to internalize the belief that you are worthy and deserving of love, regardless of external circumstances. Research suggests that self-validation is crucial for emotional well-being and can reduce the tendency to rely on others for emotional reassurance (Naor & Mayseless, 2020).

Strengthening Identity and Self-Worth Outside of Relationships

Another key aspect of overcoming relationship anxiety is strengthening your sense of identity outside of your relationship. Many people with relationship anxiety lose themselves in their partners, feeling as though their value is tied to the relationship. When you take the time to invest in your interests, hobbies, and goals, you begin to slowly build a strong sense of independence from that of your romantic life and identity.

Consider:

- exploring hobbies or passions that bring you joy.
- building strong, supportive friendships.
- setting personal goals that align with your values and interests.

As you strengthen your identity, you become less reliant on a relationship to provide validation and security. This shift can significantly reduce anxiety and increase your overall well-being.

Breaking free from relationship anxiety is not about finding the "perfect" partner who will erase all fear; it is about doing the inner work to cultivate security, trust, and resilience within yourself. Every anxious thought or reaction is an opportunity for growth. By rewiring negative thought patterns, building emotional regulation skills, and fostering self-security, you can break the cycle of anxiety and experience healthier, more fulfilling relationships.

30-Day Secure Connection Challenge

For the next 30 days, challenge yourself to take small and intentional actions that will reinforce security, trust, and emotional connection with yourself and your relationship. These daily exercises are small steps you can take to break those anxious patterns, foster mindfulness, and strengthen your bond.

Week 1: Building Self-Security (Focus on You First!)

Day 1: Write down three things you love about yourself outside of your relationship.

Day 2: Practice self-validation—pause and give yourself that reassurance instead of seeking it from your partner.

Day 3: Identify one cognitive distortion (e.g., catastrophizing, mind reading) and challenge it with facts.

Day 4: Spend at least 30 minutes doing something you enjoy *alone* (hobby, self-care, reading).

Day 5: Practice the Mindful Pause—when anxiety arises, breathe, observe, challenge, and choose your response.

Day 6: Create a personal affirmation about your worth in relationships and repeat it throughout the day.

Day 7: Reflect on how this week's self-security practices made you feel.

Week 2: Strengthening Trust and Communication (Challenge Insecurities in Your Relationship)

Day 8: Send your partner a message of appreciation without expecting an immediate response.

Day 9: When an anxious thought appears, write down two alternative, neutral explanations.

Day 10: Practice deep listening—let your partner speak without interrupting or planning your response.

Day 11: Share a small vulnerability with your partner (a worry, a goal, or something on your mind).

Day 12: If you feel triggered today, pause and ask yourself: *What is this feeling really about?*

Day 13: Give your partner space without anxiety—encourage them to enjoy something independently.

Day 14: Reflect on this week: How did challenging insecurities shift your connection?

Week 3: Replacing Anxiety With Mindfulness and Presence (Ground Yourself in the Present)

Day 15: Start the day with five minutes of deep breathing and intention-setting.

Day 16: Go for a mindful walk—focus on your senses rather than anxious thoughts.

Day 17: When you feel anxious, describe five things you can see, hear, or touch in the moment.

Day 18: Set a "no-phone hour" with your partner—focus on real presence, not digital distractions.

Day 19: Notice your body language—practice softening tension when communicating.

Day 20: Do a short guided meditation on letting go of fear and control in relationships.

Day 21: Reflect: Has mindfulness helped you feel more secure in your relationship?

Week 4: Cultivating a Secure, Loving Dynamic (Lean Into Emotional Safety)

Day 22: Express love or appreciation without worrying about how it's received.

Day 23: Identify one past anxious reaction and brainstorm how you'd handle it differently now.

Day 24: If you feel the urge to overthink, redirect your attention to a grounding activity.

Day 25: Talk about future dreams with your partner—without attaching anxiety to them.

Day 26: Practice emotional regulation by using self-soothing techniques when stress arises.

Day 27: Write a letter to your future self about the secure partner you're becoming.

Day 28: Do something spontaneous with your partner purely for joy and connection.

Day 29: Reflect on how your mindset around relationships has shifted over the past 30 days.

Day 30: Celebrate your progress—acknowledge your work and set one long-term intention for a secure relationship.

The goal of each day is not just to roll through them—it's about building a stronger foundation of security. Repeat this as many times as you want; what matters is a small, consistent, and deliberate effort.

Chapter 4:
OVERCOMING FEAR OF ABANDONMENT AND REJECTION

If you believe everyone will leave,
how can you ever feel safe in love?

–Dr. Sue Johnson

The Weight of Fear in Love

I magine falling in love but never feeling genuinely secure—you're always on edge, waiting for the other shoe to drop. Perhaps you have experienced this fear before: a delayed text sends you spiraling, an argument makes you think they might leave, or you feel an overwhelming need to earn love to keep it. This fear of abandonment and rejection is exhausting; it shapes how you engage in relationships and affects your self-perception.

But what if you could break free from it?

Understanding the origins of these fears and learning how to navigate them is crucial for building strong, lasting relationships based on trust and security. This chapter will help you recognize the roots of your fears, reshape your attachment patterns, and establish a foundation of self-worth that isn't dependent on others' approval.

Understanding the Fear of Being Left Behind— The Psychology Behind Fear of Abandonment

The fear of abandonment is a heavy, haunting experience that many people with anxious attachment live with. But this fear isn't just about the surface-level worry that someone might leave. It runs deeper—it reflects a subconscious belief that you are, at some core level, unworthy of lasting love and emotional security. This fear is not random or without cause. It has its roots in our early experiences, often formed in childhood, and can follow us into adulthood, shaping how we create bonds and interpret our relationships, regardless of whether romantic or not.

At the heart of this fear is a psychological framework known as attachment theory, developed by British psychologist John Bowlby (1969). Bowlby's work focused on the idea that the emotional bonds formed with our caregivers in childhood play a considerable role in how we interact with others as adults. Simply put, how we are treated by those who cared for us when we were young affects how we approach intimacy, love, and emotional connection in our adult relationships.

The Role of Attachment Theory in Our Fear of Abandonment

Bowlby's attachment theory identifies three primary attachment styles, each of which can explain why someone might experience an intense fear of abandonment (Cherry, 2025).

Here's a breakdown of the three types and how they influence the way we relate to others:

- **Secure attachment:** If you are consistent, responsive, and emotionally available, you likely grew up feeling safe in relationships. You probably didn't have to constantly worry about whether others would leave you because your caregivers were there when you needed them. People with a secure attachment style are generally comfortable with intimacy and independence—they know they are worthy of love and that their needs will be met in healthy relationships.

- **Anxious attachment:** If your caregivers were unpredictable—sometimes loving and responsive, other times emotionally distant or unavailable—you may have grown up feeling unsure of your place in their lives. As a result, you might have learned to cling to others out of fear that they might leave. This creates a cycle of anxiety in relationships, where you constantly worry about rejection or abandonment. You might find yourself overanalyzing your partner's actions, desperately seeking reassurance, or feeling abandoned even when everything is fine. The core belief driving anxious attachment is that "I'm not enough"—the notion that one must earn love through constant effort, and even then, love might not be guaranteed.

- **Avoidant attachment:** If your caregivers were emotionally distant, neglectful, or unavailable, you may have learned to depend on yourself, pushing others away to protect yourself from hurt. You may struggle to open up to others or feel uncomfortable with too much closeness. People with avoidant attachment styles often find it difficult to trust others or rely on them emotionally. Their fear of abandonment might manifest as emotional detachment or withdrawal. They avoid vulnerability because relying on others will only lead to disappointment.

The Cycle of Fear and Anxiety in Anxious Attachment
The emotions that an anxious person experiences can be not only consuming but also an emotional rollercoaster.

Why?

- **Inconsistent care creates uncertainty:** Your nervous system is constantly alert if you grew up with inconsistent or unpredictable care. Your caregivers might have been loving and warm one moment and distant or neglectful the next. This emotional rollercoaster leaves a lasting mark on your psyche. You learned to be hypervigilant about other people's moods, hoping that their love wouldn't suddenly withdraw. As an adult, this emotional conditioning translates into relationships, where you may constantly worry that your partner will suddenly lose interest or leave.

- **Fear of rejection becomes a self-fulfilling prophecy:** In relationships, people with anxious attachment often anticipate rejection, even when it's not a reality. They might be extra sensitive to signs that a partner is upset or pulling away, and as a result, they can become overly clingy or demanding, seeking constant reassurance. This behavior may inadvertently push others away, creating the very rejection they fear. It's a tragic cycle: fear of abandonment leads to behaviors that increase the likelihood of being abandoned.

- **Emotional regulation struggles:** When you live in a state of heightened anxiety about your relationships, it becomes challenging to regulate your emotions. The slightest sign of distance from a partner can trigger a flood of overwhelming feelings—fear, doubt, sadness, and panic. The fear of being left behind often leads to emotional dysregulation, where your emotions feel too intense to handle, and you may react in ways that you later regret. These emotional outbursts can create further tension in relationships, making you feel even more disconnected or rejected.

On top of the emotional rollercoaster, there is a deep-seated fear of being unworthy of receiving love and uncertainty about how to give love. At the root of the anxious attachment style lies a core belief that one is unworthy of love or that one's love is conditional. This belief often stems from childhood experiences where your emotional needs may not have been consistently met. Whether you experienced emotional neglect, inconsistent caregiving, or even just the absence of certain needs being acknowledged, you may have internalized the idea that love is scarce or hard to earn.

These feelings can lead to thoughts of:

- "If I don't act perfectly, they will leave."

- "I have to give and give to earn love."

- "No one will truly love me for who I am."

- "If I am not constantly available or pleasing, I will be abandoned."

These negative and undermining thoughts can create a cycle of hypervigilance and self-doubt. The anxious person will always be on alert for their partner, fearing they will leave them or reject their efforts.

There is hope, though—there is a way to change the narrative and break the cycle, which is the first step in healing the fear of abandonment.

Five ways to begin the process of breaking the cycle include:

- **Awareness:** The first step is awareness—recognizing when your fear of abandonment is triggering intense emotional reactions or unhealthy behaviors in relationships. When you feel that anxiety creeping in, pause and remind yourself that your feelings are valid, but they don't have to dictate your actions.

- **Self-compassion:** Learn to offer yourself self-compassion during moments of fear and insecurity. Remind yourself that your worth is not tied to whether someone stays or leaves and that you are worthy of love exactly as you are.

- **Challenge negative beliefs:** Identify and challenge the core beliefs that fuel your fear of abandonment. For example, instead of thinking, "I must be perfect to be loved," challenge yourself with, "I am lovable even with my imperfections." Practice reframing these negative thoughts to cultivate a healthier self-image.

- **Create secure attachments:** Try to form relationships with consistent, trustworthy, and emotionally available people. People with secure attachment styles can help you feel safer and more confident in your relationships. Practice vulnerability with these individuals by sharing your fears and emotions without fear of judgment or rejection.

- **Emotional regulation:** Work on developing emotional regulation skills. Practices like mindfulness, breathing exercises, and journaling can help you manage your anxiety and better cope with emotional distress.

The fear of abandonment is harrowing, but it doesn't define you. At its core, this fear is driven by the belief that you are unworthy of love or that love is something you have to earn through perfection. True love, however, is not conditional. It's not about achieving it—it's about being worthy of love simply because you exist.

As you begin to unravel these fears and beliefs, you'll find that you are worthy of unconditional, secure, and lasting love. It's time to stop fearing abandonment and start embracing your inherent worthiness.

How Rejection in Childhood Impacts Adult Relationships

As children, when we face and experience repeated rejection—whether through abandonment, emotional neglect, or inconsistent affection—we begin to associate this with a sense of "love" with fear. Unfortunately, this type of upbringing and relationship dynamic with our parents can have a lasting impact on our adult relationships, both emotionally and psychologically. However, don't let this discourage you—you are taking the first step and recognizing that you are anxious in love and don't want to continue down this path.

Consequences that come from rejection as a child that comes out in adulthood include:

- **Hypervigilance in relationships:** Children who have experienced rejection often become hyper-aware of their relationships. They may constantly look for signs that someone might leave them, which can create an overwhelming sense of anxiety. Research in psychology shows that this heightened sense of vigilance serves as a defense mechanism. It helps them try to predict and prevent further abandonment (Mikulincer & Shaver, 2010).

- **People-pleasing behaviors:** At a young age, a child may also develop a strong need to please others. They might go out of their way to make others happy or avoid conflict in order to prevent rejection. This behavior stems from a fear of being left alone and can lead to unhealthy relationship dynamics, where they feel they must sacrifice their own needs to maintain connections (Butler et al., 2003).

- **Fear of emotional intimacy:** Although they may crave closeness, these children often push people away before they can get hurt. This fear of emotional intimacy can lead to difficulties in forming deep, trusting adult relationships.

Studies have shown that individuals who experienced early rejection may struggle to express vulnerability in relationships, leading to a cycle of loneliness and disconnection (Collins & Read, 1990).

When we desire to break the cycle and anxious behavior, we understand the impact our upbringing has on our present. Addressing these fears, doubts, and insecurities in a safe and nurturing environment can help heal and improve our relationship dynamics in a healthy and assertive manner.

Sarah's Story
Sarah grew up in a home where love felt conditional. If she performed well in school, she was praised. If she made mistakes, affection was withdrawn. As an adult, she found herself in relationships where she felt she had to "earn" love, overextending herself to avoid rejection.

When a partner needed space, she saw it as a sign they were losing interest, triggering panic.

Recognizing these patterns is the first step toward healing.

The Connection Between Abandonment Fears and Codependency
Codependency is a pattern where self-worth is tied to others' approval (Keng et al., 2011). Those with deep fears of rejection often develop codependent tendencies, meaning they:

- They put their partner's needs above their own, even when unhealthy.

- They struggle to say "no" for fear of losing the relationship.

- They feel anxious when their partner is not immediately available.

Overcoming codependency requires breaking the belief that our worth depends on someone else staying.

It can be hard to navigate healthy relationships when one struggles with codependency. As mentioned, they will constantly put their partner's needs above their own, even if it may be detrimental to their own emotional and mental well-being. Along with not being able to maintain healthy boundaries, someone struggling with codependency may experience higher levels of anxiety, especially during long periods of being away from their partner. Their absence can trigger significant distress, whether due to work commitments, social activities, or other obligations. This anxiety is frequently rooted in the belief that their value is directly linked to their availability and closeness to their partner, making it challenging for them to function independently.

Jason's Story of Codependency
Jason always found himself in relationships where he felt responsible for his partner's happiness. If his girlfriend was upset, he took it personally and would go to extreme lengths to "fix" the situation.

He realized that his need to avoid conflict came from childhood experiences where expressing emotions led to rejection.

Develop Secure Relationship Habits

Fear of abandonment often leads to a cycle of self-sabotage in our relationships. When we struggle with these fears, we may pull a yo-yo move, where we crave closeness one moment and then withdraw the next, scared of being too vulnerable. This push-pull dynamic serves as a coping mechanism to manage and protect ourselves from potential rejection, but it ultimately prevents true intimacy. To modify this behavior, we first need to understand our triggers and recognize what a secure connection looks and feels like.

Communicating Without Fear of Rejection

The sad reality for many with anxious attachment tendencies is the fear of abandonment. These feelings, unfortunately, often lead to them silently suffering—they avoid bringing up their needs because they fear pushing their partner away. However, secure relationships require healthy communication.

Holding in your feelings does not help you or your partner. Here are three things you can do to express and communicate your needs effectively.

1. **Identify what you need**: Instead of assuming your partner should "just know," clarify what you need emotionally.

2. **Use 'I' statements**: Say, *"I feel anxious when we don't talk about plans"* instead of *"You never make me a priority."*

3. **Separate fear from reality**: Before reacting, ask: *Is my fear based on past experiences, or is it really happening now?*

Expressing your needs effectively is essential for fostering healthy relationships, but it must be paired with setting healthy boundaries to maintain emotional well-being and connection.

It's important to establish healthy boundaries while also maintaining a healthy connection. Doing this will create emotional safety and give you a sense of self-respect, preventing the loss of your identity in relationships.

What does an unhealthy boundary look like? The moment you say, "I'll do anything to keep this person in my life, even if it means ignoring my own needs." This harmful and narrow mindset often leads to resentment and emotional burnout. Conversely, a healthy boundary reflects balance: "I deserve to have my needs met while respecting my partner's space." This encourages mutual respect, ensuring both parties feel heard and valued.

Establishing healthy boundaries requires clear communication about your needs while remaining open to the needs of others. Boundaries are not walls; they are guidelines that protect your emotional space. By maintaining them, you can thrive personally and nurture strong connections, leading to more fulfilling and respectful relationships.

Strengthening Self-Worth and Independence

Building confidence outside of relationships is important for maintaining a healthy sense of self-worth. One common misconception is that our value decreases when our partner or someone, such as a friend or family member, leaves. This belief can result in one feeling a sense of inadequacy or sadness. However, recognizing that we are inherently worthy of love and respect, regardless of our relationship status, is a powerful step in boosting self-assurance. One effective way to nurture this belief is through self-affirmation.

Psychological research supports the idea that challenging negative self-talk can improve self-esteem (Cohen & Sherman, 2014). When feelings of doubt arise, affirmations like "I am worthy of love, even when I am alone" can help counteract harmful thoughts.

Such statements encourage us to reaffirm our identity and values, which helps build a stronger, more resilient sense of self. Another effective strategy is to pursue individual interests. Engaging in hobbies, building friendships, or setting goals outside of romantic relationships enables us to create a solid foundation for self-worth that doesn't rely on others. Independence in these areas leads to more fulfilling connections and a deeper understanding of our preferences and passions. Whether painting, hiking, or learning a new instrument, developing these interests empowers us to define who we are without needing external validation. Research shows that individuals who engage in activities that bring them joy tend to report higher levels of satisfaction and well-being (Ryan & Deci, 2000).

Embracing solitude can contribute significantly to building self-worth. Given today's fast-paced, overly interconnected world, being alone can sometimes feel intimidating. However, solitude offers a valuable opportunity for self-growth when viewed positively. Instead of seeing alone time as a void, we can consider it a chance to discover what truly brings us happiness.

This idea aligns with intrinsic motivation theory, which suggests that engaging in activities for their own sake creates a greater sense of satisfaction(Ryan & Deci, 2000). Solitude also offers an opportunity for reflection. Taking time to think about personal goals and aspirations helps clarify what we truly want from life. This process allows us to assess our progress and adjust our efforts accordingly. Engaging in introspective practices, such as journaling or meditation, can enhance emotional awareness and deepen self-understanding. Research by Choi et al. (2019) supports this, demonstrating that such practices contribute to a deeper understanding of one's emotions.

Developing self-sufficiency is one of the most empowering outcomes of embracing solitude. When we learn to rely on ourselves for emotional support, we build resilience and a sense of control over our lives. A study by Mohammadkhani et al. (2017) found that individuals who felt more self-sufficient reported lower anxiety levels and better psychological well-being. By nurturing our independence, we reinforce our self-worth, making it less likely to be affected by external circumstances.

Building confidence outside relationships involves a multifaceted approach focused on self-affirmation, pursuing personal interests, embracing solitude, and cultivating self-sufficiency. This journey leads to greater self-discovery and growth. By understanding our intrinsic value and cultivating a fulfilling life outside of relationships, we enhance our self-esteem and become better partners and friends. Everyone deserves to feel valued and fulfilled in their own right. Nurturing these aspects of our lives can help us achieve a deeper sense of happiness and contentment.

Remember, You Are Not Defined by Past Rejection

Overcoming the fear of abandonment means learning to trust yourself. You do not have to be trapped in cycles of anxiety and codependency. Instead, you can develop secure, healthy connections by:

- Recognizing how past experiences shape your fears.

- Rewiring negative thought patterns.

- Building self-worth from within.

Call to Action: The Letter to Your Younger Self Exercise

To truly heal, it's important to offer yourself the compassion you might not have received growing up.

Take 10-15 minutes to write a letter to your younger self, offering reassurance, love, and encouragement.

Steps:

1. Address yourself as a child: Begin with *"Dear [Your Name], I know you've felt afraid of being left behind..."*

2. Acknowledge past pain: Write about the experiences that made you feel unworthy.

3. Offer reassurance: Tell your younger self what you needed to hear.

4. Express hope: Remember that love is available, and you are enough.

By completing this exercise, you are taking a powerful step toward breaking the cycle of abandonment fears and creating a secure future.

Chapter 5:
COMMUNICATING EFFECTIVELY IN RELATIONSHIPS

What if speaking your needs didn't push people away—but brought them closer?

–Dr. Marshall Rosenberg

Have you ever found yourself holding back your true feelings, worried that opening up might make you seem needy or could push someone away? This is a common struggle for many with anxious attachments.

You might have even attempted to share what's on your mind, only to feel unheard or misunderstood. Communicating your feelings and thoughts can feel daunting, especially when the fear of abandonment or rejection looms.

But what if you could use voice as a bridge, not a barrier? Imagine the possibilities when it comes to expressing your truth, which could strengthen your relationship and bring you closer to those you care about. When you share your feelings openly and honestly, you invite understanding and connection. Instead of ending love, your vulnerability can deepen it in ways you never thought possible. What if these moments of honesty could be the key to cultivating more authentic and fulfilling relationships?

Speaking Up Without Pushing Love Away

Effective communication isn't about saying everything perfectly—it's about showing up with honesty and clarity. Many of us learned to bottle things up or explode when emotions run high. We weren't taught how to calmly say, "I need reassurance," or how to hear someone else's pain without getting defensive. That's okay. We can learn now.

By breaking down the communication habits that build closeness and trust, one can learn how to express their needs with confidence, listen without assuming the worst, and handle conflict in ways that strengthen relationships rather than tear them apart.

The truth is, healthy communication isn't just a skill—it's a form of self-love. It says, "I matter. You matter. Our connection matters." Learning to communicate effectively doesn't just change your relationships but your life.

Ready? Let's begin.

Speaking Without Anxiety

If you have an anxious attachment style, you've probably had this thought before: *"If I speak up, they'll think I'm too needy."* Or maybe, *"If I ask for reassurance, they'll get tired of me and leave."* These thoughts can be incredibly loud and often stop you from expressing what you truly feel or need in a relationship.

Here's the truth: *your needs are not a burden.*

Desiring closeness, reassurance, or emotional connection is human. Everyone needs these things. But when you've grown up in an environment where your needs weren't consistently met—or worse, were dismissed—you might've learned that asking for anything puts love at risk. So, you stay quiet. You hold it in. You pretend you're fine.

But holding back doesn't protect the relationship—it creates a silent storm inside you.

Those feelings don't go away when you don't express what you need. They build up. The longer you stay silent, the more you second-guess yourself, replay conversations, and try to manage everything internally. Eventually, all that bottled-up anxiety can turn into resentment, self-blame, or emotional outbursts that confuse your partner—and leave you feeling worse.

You deserve to be heard. And there's a way to speak your truth without pushing love away.

Start small. You don't have to pour your heart out all at once. Try naming how you feel in the moment. For example:

- *"Hey, I noticed I've been feeling a little anxious lately. Can we check in for a few minutes?"*

- *"Sometimes I get caught in my head and start assuming things. I'd love to talk about how we're doing."*

Speaking in this manner helps keep the conversation grounded in connection, not conflict. It opens the door without sounding like a demand.

And remember: how someone responds to your needs tells you a lot about the relationship. Emotionally healthy partners won't be scared off by your honesty. They'll want to understand and meet you where you are. Your vulnerability gives them the chance to show up with care.

If someone labels your needs as "too much," that's not a reflection of your worth—it's a sign they may not be capable of offering the kind of connection you deserve.

So let's rewrite the inner script. Instead of:

- *"I'll push them away if I say this,"* try:
- *"I'm building trust by being honest."*

Instead of:

- *"They'll think I'm needy,"* try:

- *"My needs matter, and I can express them clearly."*

Speaking without anxiety isn't about being perfect—it's about being real.

The more you practice, the easier it gets. And over time, you'll notice that speaking up brings you closer to the secure, healthy love you've been looking for—not further away from it.

Practice Time—Speaking Confidently

Use this four-step guide whenever you feel anxious in a relationship and want to speak up clearly and calmly.

1. Notice the Trigger

Think of a recent moment you felt anxious (e.g., a delayed text or a canceled plan).

"I felt anxious when they didn't reply last night."

2. Name the Emotion and Need

Ask yourself, *"What was I really feeling? What did I need in that moment?"*

"I felt insecure and needed reassurance."

3. Create a Gentle Message

Use this formula:

"When [event], I felt [emotion], and I think I needed [need]. Could we [request]?"

"When I didn't hear from you, I felt anxious. I think I just needed a little reassurance. Could we check in more regularly?"

4. Practice Out Loud
Say it in the mirror or to yourself. This builds confidence and teaches your nervous system that it's safe to speak up.

Your needs are valid. Expressing them isn't being "too much"—it's building healthier, more secure love.

Overcoming the Fear of Being "Too Much"
When a partner who grew up in a stable and secure household dates someone with these feelings, they may not realize that their anxieties stem from their upbringing. People who experience anxious attachments often grow up in environments where their emotions are dismissed or punished. They would be told they were being dramatic, sensitive, or needy. As a result, they may have learned that expressing themselves leads to rejection.

They understand that healthy relationships thrive on open communication; however, they can struggle to achieve and practice this.

On a good day, communication can be challenging for even those who aren't anxious; however, sharing our feelings isn't a burden—it's an invitation to be known.

Elena's Story

Elena always felt afraid to tell her partner when she was feeling insecure. She worried it would make her look unstable. So instead of saying, "I'm feeling anxious—can we talk?" she'd withdraw or become passive-aggressive. Eventually, her partner felt confused and overwhelmed.

When Elena finally learned to express her needs calmly, her partner responded with more empathy, not less.

Expressing Our Needs in a Confident, Non-Clingy Way

Here are a few steps for clear, anxiety-free communication:

- **Pause and check-in:** What do I need now—comfort, clarity, connection?

- **Use 'I' statements:** Instead of accusing ("You never listen"), express your experience ("I feel unheard when...")

- **Be specific:** General complaints feel overwhelming. Specific needs create clarity.

- **Keep it grounded:** Speak from a calm, grounded place—not from panic.

How to Express Yourself in a Calm, Clear Way

Finding the words to express ourselves that don't come across as anxious, frightened, or unsure can be hard.

Here are some statements that can help start the conversation.

- "I've been feeling anxious lately and could use reassurance from you. Is this a good time to talk?"

- "When plans change, and I don't hear from you, I sometimes feel insecure. I know that's my stuff, but it helps me to know what's going on."

- "I'm not asking you to fix anything—I just want to share how I'm feeling."

Understanding Your Partner Through Active Listening

What we often forget about being an effective communicator is that it also involves being an active listener. This means fully concentrating on what your partner is saying without interruptions or preconceived notions. For individuals with fears of abandonment, practicing active listening and responding with empathy can be especially challenging.

This is especially important when it comes to understanding your partner's feelings and perspectives. By practicing empathy, you can foster a supportive environment that alleviates anxieties and strengthens your connection.

How to Listen Without Assuming Rejection

If you have an anxious attachment style, chances are your nervous system is always on high alert. Your brain is wired to detect any sign—real or imagined—that love might be slipping away. You're not overreacting; you're reacting from a place of deeply learned survival. Psychologist Dr. Sue Johnson, founder of Emotionally Focused Therapy, explains that attachment needs are biological, not just emotional. When we feel disconnected from someone we care about, the brain actually lights up in areas associated with physical pain (Johnson, 2004).

When someone says, *"I need space,"* your brain might translate that to *"They're pulling away... I'm being rejected."* But here's the reframe: *What if "I need space" really just means... "I need space"?* Nothing more. No hidden meaning. No threat. Just a person honoring their needs in the moment.

This is where the power of slowing down comes in.

When your fear of abandonment kicks in, pause. Take a deep breath and give yourself a second to step back from your assumptions. Instead of jumping to conclusions, get curious.

Curiosity is your best tool for connection. Here are some statements you can use to engage your partner in a meaningful and fruitful conversation.

- *"I'm really interested in your perspective. Can you tell me more about how you feel?"*

- *"I'd love to understand your thoughts better. What led you to that decision?"*

- *"What's been on your mind lately? I'd love to hear more."*

- *"How did you arrive at that conclusion? I'm curious about your process."*

- *"Can you share more about your experience? I want to understand. "*Understanding your own attachment style is just as important as understanding.

These questions are open-ended rather than interrogative. They are invitational and use open and curious language. You are allowing the other person to open up in a safe and nonjudgmental environment. For the anxious person, it also gives you an opportunity to regulate your emotions before jumping to engaging in worst-case conclusions.

Another helpful strategy? Name what you're feeling—gently. You might say:

- *"I noticed I started feeling anxious after what you said. I know that's my stuff, but I just wanted to share it with you."*

This kind of honest, non-blaming communication allows space for both people in the relationship to feel seen and safe. It bridges the gap instead of widening it.

Listening without assuming rejection is a skill; like any skill, it takes time to build. But with practice, you'll notice a shift: fewer spirals, fewer misread cues, and a more real, grounded connection.

At the heart of anxious attachment isn't just fear—it's a deep desire to be understood. Learning to listen with curiosity instead of fear brings you one step closer to the secure love you've always wanted.

It's Not Just Your Attachment Style—Recognizing Your Partner's Style

Understanding your own attachment style is just as important as understanding your partner's style. Doing this can help foster a deeper and more compassionate relationship. We all have our own unique experiences, especially when it comes to life and love, which impact our current and future relationships. By recognizing these styles, you can navigate your relationship with more empathy and patience, reducing misunderstandings and emotional distress.

Avoidant partners often prioritize independence and may feel overwhelmed when they sense too much emotional intensity. They frequently seek out space, although an anxious partner may interpret this as rejection. This isn't the case; they simply seek a moment to be and ground themselves.

Conversely, secure partners often demonstrate more consistency and emotional availability. The trouble with secure partners is that if you are an anxious partner and are not accustomed to this type of relationship or dynamic, it can be both overwhelming and underwhelming.

Conflict Resolution Strategies for Anxious Partners

When it comes to anxious partners, recognizing your emotional triggers and having strategies to address these triggers can result in healthier relationships and interactions.

Here are a few strategies to help when you find yourself in a situation of conflict:

- **Take space before reacting:** Give yourself time to process your emotions before responding to triggering situations. This could involve journaling, taking deep breaths, or walking.

- **Stay in the present:** Focus on the current issue rather than revisiting past conflicts. This helps prevent escalation and keeps the conversation constructive.

- **Use repair attempts:** If something you say doesn't go well, acknowledge it with phrases like, "That didn't come out right—can I try again?" This shows your commitment to effective communication.

- **Name what's underneath:** Often, our anger can mask deeper feelings of fear or hurt. Acknowledging this by saying something like, "I got defensive because I felt unimportant," can help both partners understand the root of the issue and facilitate healing.

Using these strategies or having a game plan for your attachment styles and communication can foster a more supportive and loving relationship, both with your potential partner and with yourself.

Why Boundaries Foster Security, Not Distance

Often, we fear that by setting boundaries with those in our lives, we will push them away. The reality is that the opposite is true. Boundaries establish a sense of emotional security and safety while also teaching others how to love and respect us.

Think of your boundary as a fence—not a wall. It lets people know where the door is and how to enter in a way that honors your space.

Jordan's Story
Jordan used to say yes to everything his boyfriend asked, even when he was exhausted. He feared saying no would lead to a breakup, but instead of building closeness, this left Jordan resentful. When he started saying, "I need to recharge tonight. Can we hang out tomorrow?" His boyfriend respected his honesty, and their connection grew stronger.

Saying "No" Guilt Free and Without Fear
Knowing how and when to say "no" is an important lesson to learn, as it is a huge proponent in establishing our boundaries (Hinton et al., 2020).

Here are a few ways you can say "no" and not feel guilty about doing it:

- **Start with gratitude:** Acknowledge appreciation for the offer when declining a request. This softens the refusal and shows respect for the other person's request.

  Example: "Thank you so much for inviting me to dinner! I really appreciate it, but I need to decline this time."

- **Use "I" statements:** Frame your response from your perspective to help reduce defensiveness in the other person.

  Example: "I'm feeling overwhelmed and need time to myself right now. I can't commit to that project at the moment."

- **Be honest about your limitations:** Sharing your true reasons can foster understanding.

  Example: "I'm on a tight deadline this week, so I won't be able to join the team for drinks after work."

- **Offer alternatives:** Suggest a future time to connect or propose a different activity if appropriate.

  Example: "I can't make it to the movie this weekend, but I'd love to catch up over coffee next week!"

- **Practice assertiveness:** Remember, it's okay to prioritize your needs without having to justify extensively.

  Example: "No, I can't help you with that right now. I need to focus on my own commitments."

While we can do our part to establish and stand our ground, there will be times when people do not respect our boundaries. This can be difficult to navigate.

What to Do When Boundaries Are Violated
Here are a few tips on handling situations when our boundaries are violated.

- **Acknowledge your feelings**: Allow yourself to feel upset or frustrated when your boundaries are crossed. It's valid to have those emotions.

  Example: "I felt really uncomfortable when you didn't respect my request about personal space."

- **Communicate clearly and calmly:** Address the boundary that has been violated directly but without aggression. Use a calm tone to discuss the situation.

  Example: "I want to remind you that I mentioned I need quiet time after work. When that's not respected, it makes things difficult for me."

- **Set or reiterate consequences:** This helps others understand the importance of your boundaries.

Example: "If this continues to happen, I'll need to take a step back from our conversations until it's resolved."

- **Be prepared to walk away:** Emphasize that you will prioritize your well-being.

  Example: "I have to protect my boundaries, and if they're not respected, I might not engage as much moving forward."

- **Seek resolution**: Encourage an opportunity to communicate about improving respect for your boundaries moving forward.

  Example: "Can we discuss how to ensure our needs are met in this relationship?"

Communication is Love in Action

When we think of love, we often picture big, romantic gestures—flowers, long talks under the stars, heartfelt "I love you's." However, one of the most powerful expressions of love is much quieter and far more important: clear, honest communication.

When you suffer from anxious attachment, communication can feel risky. You might worry that speaking your truth will drive people away. Maybe you've had experiences where expressing your needs was met with rejection, withdrawal, or judgment. Over time, this teaches you to stay quiet, tiptoe around discomfort, and hope that others will just *know* what you need. But the truth is—they won't.

Healthy relationships aren't built on guesswork. They're built on open conversations, where both people feel safe to be genuine.

De Netto et al. (2021) believe open and intentional communication fosters greater relationship satisfaction, emotional closeness, and trust. In other words, talking about your feelings, fears, boundaries, and desires is not too much. It's essential.

And here's the beautiful part: every time you express yourself clearly, you're not just building a better relationship—you're showing up as your most authentic self.

You stop pretending. You stop shrinking. You stop molding yourself into what you *think* others want to feel safe.

Instead, you allow your whole self to be seen. And that is love in action—not just toward others, but toward *yourself.*

It's okay to take space.

It's okay to ask for clarity.

It's okay to say, "That didn't sit right with me."

It's okay to say, "I need some reassurance."

Often, people with anxious attachment feel like they must always earn love by being agreeable, available, or easygoing. But secure love doesn't work that way. Secure love invites your truth to the table—not just your people-pleasing side.

It's worth repeating and remembering: you can ask for what you need.

Let go of the idea that love means never having conflict or discomfort. Love deepens when two people navigate those uncomfortable moments *together*—with honesty, care, and mutual respect.

So speak up, even if your voice shakes. Take space when you need to recharge. Say what matters to you, even if it feels vulnerable.

You don't have to be perfect to be loved—you have to be real. Because communication, at its core, is love in motion. It says, *"I care enough about this relationship to be honest."* And that's what creates safety. That's what creates a secure connection.

Whenever you express your truth, you're not pushing someone away—you're inviting them into a relationship based on *truth,* not fear.

And if someone can't meet you there? That doesn't mean you're too much. It just means they weren't ready for the kind of love you're learning to give—and deserve to receive.

Practicing Assertive Communication

Looking to improve or practice how to communicate assertively?

Here are some ways you can practice communicating assertively:

Role-Playing Scenarios
With a trusted friend, practice situations where you need to assert yourself. This can build confidence.

Example: Role-play saying no to a friend who continually asks for favors you're uncomfortable doing.

- Set specific goals: Identify areas where you want to practice assertive communication.

  Example: "This week, I will say no to at least one request that doesn't serve me."

- **Use positive affirmations:** Remind yourself that asserting your needs is a healthy practice and that it's okay to prioritize your well-being.

  Example: "My needs are important, and I have the right to express them."

- **Seek feedback:** After having a conversation, ask for feedback from the person involved to understand how your communication was perceived.

  Example: "I expressed my need clearly, how did that come off to you?"

Taking the time to be aware of how one communicates can help not only establish and set clear boundaries but will further enhance and improve your communication.

Communication is a key factor in nurturing relationships between an anxious person and not.

QUIZ: How Strong Are Your Communication Skills?

Answer Yes or No to the following statements:

1. I often hesitate to express my needs in relationships.

2. I feel guilty when I say no.

3. I tend to assume the worst when my partner is quiet or distant.

4. I use 'I' statements when discussing difficult topics.

5. I try to understand where the other person is coming from.

6. I can set and enforce boundaries without shutting down.

7. I respond rather than react in emotionally charged conversations.

Results:

Mostly Yes: You're building strong communication skills! Keep practicing.

Mostly No: That's okay—now you know where to focus. Use this chapter as your guide.

Reflective Prompts

Remember that self-awareness will play a significant part in addressing and handling our anxious attachment styles.

One way to do this is through journaling and reflection. Here are some prompts to help you reflect on your previous communication styles. Be honest with yourself and allow vulnerability to be part of your journey to self-discovery, awareness, and happiness.

- When was a time I communicated clearly, and it went well?

- What made it go well?

- Where do I still feel nervous to speak up?

- What support would help me become more confident in sharing my truth?

Chapter 6:
HEALING THROUGH SELF-LOVE AND INNER WORK

Healing attachment anxiety starts with loving yourself the way you want to be loved.

–Dr. Nicole LePera

When we discuss healing from attachment anxiety, it's easy to concentrate on our relationships with others—improving communication, feeling secure in love, or finding the right partner. However, one relationship sets the tone for all others: our relationship with ourselves. If you have ever sought someone to make you feel whole, secure, or worthy, know you are not alone. Many people with anxious attachment styles learned early on that love is something to be earned or chased. However, true healing does not come from finally being chosen by someone else; it comes from choosing ourselves—again and again.

This chapter will explore what it means to heal from the inside out. We'll look at how to let go of the emotional baggage we carry from past relationships. We will utilize various exercises, affirmations, and real-world strategies rooted in psychology to help you return to the fundamental truth: *you are already enough.*

The Relationship That Shapes Them All— Reparenting Our Inner Child

Attachment wounds are often formed in childhood, shaped by how caregivers responded—or didn't respond—to our emotional needs. According to Bowlby's Attachment Theory (1969), early attachment experiences shape our internal working models—the beliefs we carry about ourselves, others, and relationships. If you experienced inconsistency, neglect, or emotional invalidation, your inner child may have learned that love is uncertain or conditional.

Reparenting is the act of giving your inner child the support, validation, and love that may have been missing. It's about showing up for yourself in the way you always needed someone else to.

For example, Jess grew up in a household where emotions were seen as weaknesses. When she cried or expressed fear, she was told to toughen up. As an adult, Jess often suppressed her feelings, believing they made her unlovable.

Through reparenting, Jess began to validate her own emotions. When she felt sad, she practiced saying, "It's okay to feel this. I'm here for you." This slight shift helped Jess become more emotionally grounded and self-loving.

Reflect: Think back to a moment from childhood when you felt scared, rejected, or invisible. What would that version of you have needed to hear?

Affirmations and Exercises for Self-Nurturing

Healing anxious attachment takes more than insight—it takes kindness, especially the kind you give to yourself. You may have developed a harsh inner critic when your inner world has been shaped by fear of abandonment, inconsistent love, or self-doubt.

That voice might say things like:

- "You're too needy."
- "They'll leave if you speak up."
- "You're not enough."

Over time, this inner dialogue becomes automatic. But here's the good news: you can retrain it. You can teach your inner voice to speak with care, warmth, and safety—just as a nurturing parent would.

This process is often referred to as reparenting—giving yourself the validation, support, and emotional safety you may not have consistently received growing up. One gentle but powerful way to do this is through affirmations and self-dialogue.

As psychologist Kernis (2003) explains, self-affirmation practices can increase self-esteem and reduce the emotional intensity of perceived rejection. In short, affirmations help shift you from self-criticism to self-compassion.

Exercise: Write a letter to your inner child.
Begin with "Dear little me..." and express love, validation, and protection. Acknowledge their pain. Reassure your inner child that they are not alone anymore, that they are enough, and that their feelings matter.

Practicing Self-Forgiveness
While we would like to believe that healing is straightforward, the truth is it is not. Healing isn't linear. We all make mistakes and fall into old patterns. Self-forgiveness allows you to release guilt so you can grow. According to Hall and Fincham (2005), forgiving oneself promotes emotional well-being and reduces shame.

Are you ready to forgive yourself? Try saying the following out loud: "I forgive myself for the times I didn't know how to protect or value myself. I was surviving."

Cultivating Self-Compassion
Cultivating self-compassion is especially important for someone with an anxious attachment style because it helps soothe the deep fear of abandonment and not being "good enough" in relationships. Individuals with

anxious attachment often feel overly worried about their partner's love and approval. They may constantly seek reassurance or feel hurt by minor signs of distance. These reactions come from early relationships where love may have felt inconsistent or uncertain.

Psychologically, anxious attachment is tied to a sensitive nervous system and a tendency to misread neutral situations as threatening. Self-compassion helps interrupt this cycle. Instead of harsh self-judgment ("I'm too needy," "No one will stay with me"), self-compassion invites kindness: "It's okay to feel this way," or "I'm struggling, and that's human." This calming inner voice helps regulate emotions, lowers stress, and creates a sense of emotional safety from within.

According to psychologist Kristin Neff, self-compassion comprises three main parts: self-kindness, mindfulness, and shared humanity (Neff, 2003). Self-kindness helps soften the inner critic for anxious individuals. Mindfulness creates space to observe emotions without getting overwhelmed. Common humanity reminds them that they're not alone in their fears—many people feel this way.

When someone with anxious attachment learns to treat themselves compassionately, they become less dependent on others for validation. Their relationships improve because they're not acting out of fear or desperation. They can express their needs calmly and trust that they're worthy of love, even when things aren't perfect. Over time, self-compassion can help shift attachment patterns toward a more secure style, where love feels safer and more stable.

Overcoming Self-Criticism and Perfectionism

Self-criticism often starts early. It can become a means of survival for many of us, especially those with anxious attachment. If love in childhood felt inconsistent, conditional, or unpredictable, we learned to blame *ourselves* for the pain. The thinking often goes: *If I can just be better, quieter, more helpful, less emotional... maybe then they'll stay. Perhaps then I'll be enough.*

In this way, self-criticism becomes a coping mechanism—a form of protection. It gives us a false sense of control. We may prevent rejection if we can spot every flaw before someone else does. But over time, that harsh inner voice stops helping and starts hurting. It becomes a wall that keeps us from growing, connecting, and fully accepting ourselves.

According to Dr. Kristin Neff (2003), a leading researcher in the field of self-compassion, healing begins when we learn to treat ourselves the way we'd treat a dear friend—*with kindness, patience, and understanding*, especially when we're struggling. Self-compassion is not letting yourself off the hook but learning to care for yourself through the hard moments rather than punishing yourself for them.

Why Self-Criticism Feels Safer (But Isn't)

If you have an anxious attachment style, you've likely internalized the belief that you need to earn love by being perfect, pleasing, or putting others first. Self-criticism becomes the tool you use to "fix" yourself before someone else finds you flawed and leaves.

But here's the truth: healing doesn't happen in perfection but in self-acceptance. When we constantly criticize ourselves, we're stuck in survival mode, always bracing for abandonment. Self-compassion, conversely, signals to your nervous system that you're safe, seen, and okay—even when things aren't perfect.

Dr. Kristin Neff's (2023) work on self-compassion highlights three key components that are essential to healing and emotional well-being.

The first component counters the internal critic by treating yourself with warmth and understanding during moments of suffering or failure rather than resorting to harsh self-judgment. This gentle approach helps counter the internal criticism that many anxiously attached individuals struggle with. The second component is common humanity, which involves recognizing that suffering and imperfection are universal experiences. It reminds you that you're not alone in your struggles and that everyone, regardless of their attachment style, faces challenges and setbacks. Lastly, mindfulness is the third element, which entails holding your thoughts and emotions with balanced awareness. Instead of ignoring or exaggerating your feelings, mindfulness allows you to observe your emotional experience without judgment, fostering a sense of acceptance and clarity.

Together, these three components—self-kindness, common humanity, and mindfulness—create a powerful antidote to the anxiety and self-criticism that often dominate the inner world of individuals with anxious attachment. They help shift the focus from self-blame and fear to self-compassion, allowing for healing, growth, and healthier emotional connections.

Embracing Flaws and Imperfections

Let's face it: perfectionism is exhausting. It's a constant, unrelenting pursuit of an ideal that's impossible to sustain, and for those with anxious attachment, it often feels like a requirement for love and acceptance. At its core, perfectionism is driven by fear—the fear of not being enough, of being rejected, or of losing someone important. The belief often runs deep for anxiously attached individuals: *"If I can just be perfect—if I can meet everyone's needs and never make mistakes—then I won't be abandoned."* But this belief, though common, is flawed. It keeps you stuck in a cycle of self-doubt, burnout, and anxiety.

Psychologically, perfectionism is linked to an increased risk of anxiety and depression. Dr. Brené Brown (2014), a researcher on vulnerability and shame, has shown that perfectionism is often rooted in the fear of being unworthy or of failing to meet the expectations of others. She explains that perfectionism doesn't protect us from shame; it *reinforces it* by creating a never-ending bar that can never truly be reached. As a result, anxious attachment styles, which are already characterized by the fear of abandonment and difficulty trusting others, can exacerbate these feelings of inadequacy when perfection is the standard to live up to.

The truth is nobody connects with perfection. Authentic, meaningful relationships are built on vulnerability, honesty, and the willingness to show up as you are, imperfections. Perfection might seem like a way to avoid rejection, but it prevents real connection. When you're constantly trying to present a flawless version of yourself, you're not allowing others to see your true self—the messy, imperfect, and very human part of you that others can relate to. Carl Rogers, a pioneer in humanistic psychology, argued that true self-acceptance occurs when we embrace all parts of ourselves, including our flaws. Only then can we experience genuine intimacy with others.

Flaws are not failures; they are entry points for connection. When you embrace your imperfections, you allow yourself to be vulnerable, and vulnerability is the gateway to deep, authentic relationships. Instead of fearing rejection, you begin to invite deeper understanding. By showing up as you are, without the facade of perfection, you create space for others to do the same. This leads to more genuine and lasting connections, where love is not conditional on your ability to be flawless but on your ability to be real.

Research (Kegan, 2009)has shown that relationship authenticity leads to greater emotional support and closeness. According to studies by Robert Kegan and others, individuals who embrace their authentic selves tend to experience higher levels of relational satisfaction because they can be open, honest, and vulnerable without the weight of maintaining a perfect persona. When you let go of the need to be perfect, you allow yourself to experience greater emotional freedom and form more secure, balanced attachments with others.

Allowing yourself to be fully seen, flaws and all is not only a way to heal your own emotional wounds, but it also invites others to show up more authentically. As you embrace your flaws, you create a ripple effect, encouraging those around you to let go of their pretenses and engage in relationships grounded in authenticity and mutual vulnerability. Ultimately, this is where true love and belonging are found—not in perfection but in the courage to be imperfect together.

By learning to accept your flaws, you can shift from a mindset of fear and rejection to one of self-compassion and connection. The more you practice this, the easier it becomes to show up authentically in your relationships, allowing love to flow freely—not because you are perfect, but because you are perfectly human.

Developing a Daily Self-Care Routine
Self-care is about consistency, not luxury. So often, people perceive self-care as bubble baths and spa days, but at its core, it's about building daily habits that support your mental, emotional, and physical well-being, especially when you have an anxious attachment style.

When you are anxiously attached, you often struggle with emotional regulation. The nervous system is wired to be on high alert for signs of disconnection or rejection, which can create a cycle of anxiety, overthinking, and emotional burnout. Research in *Health Psychology* (Pressman et al., 2009) highlights that consistent self-care practices—such as getting enough sleep, exercising, journaling, or pausing to breathe—can lower stress levels and build emotional resilience. This means you're better able to handle challenges without spiraling into fear or self-doubt.

For someone with anxious attachment, developing a *daily* self-care routine is about grounding oneself. It teaches your body and mind that *you* can be your own safe space. You're not just waiting for someone else to regulate your emotions—you're learning how to do it for yourself.

Self-care isn't just about you, despite it being called self-care. The benefits go beyond you because when you're calmer and more centered, you're less likely to act out of anxiety in relationships. That means fewer fights, less clinginess or emotional reactivity, and more balanced communication. You can show up with a clearer mind and a fuller heart.

Physically, consistent self-care can help reduce cortisol (the stress hormone), improve sleep, boost immunity, and support overall health. Emotionally, it builds confidence and inner security. Mentally, it helps you shift from survival mode to a more peaceful, connected way of living.

Self-care isn't selfish—it's essential. Especially for someone with anxious attachment, it's the daily act of reminding yourself: *I am safe. I am enough. I've got me.*

Design Your Routine Using These Areas:
- **Emotional:** journaling, therapy, affirmations
- **Physical:** rest, hydration, movement
- **Spiritual/Mental:** nature, art, meditation

Prompt: Asking yourself, *"What do I need to feel safe and supported today?"* will help you stay grounded and establish and maintain your boundaries and limitations.

Releasing Resentment and Past Relationship Pain

Let's be real: letting go is *hard*. When someone's hurt you—whether it was a past partner, a parent, or someone you trusted deeply—your heart remembers. And if you have an anxious attachment style, those memories don't fade into the background. They *linger*. They whisper, "What if it happens again?" or "You're not safe unless you're on high alert."

Holding onto pain can feel like protection. It's your brain's way of saying, *"Never again."* But here's the truth: the longer we hold onto that pain, the heavier it becomes. Over time, it stops protecting us and begins to trap us. It keeps us stuck in patterns that replay the same old wounds repeatedly.

The good news is that healing is absolutely possible. The key thing is that it begins with forgiveness—not necessarily for *them*, but for *you*.

According to a study by Witvliet et al. (2001), practicing forgiveness can reduce anxiety, improve mental health, and even have physical benefits such as lower blood pressure. That's huge. Forgiveness isn't about saying what happened was okay—it's about saying, *"I deserve peace more than I deserve to keep hurting."*

When you release resentment, you make room for new experiences. You stop reacting to your partner as if they're your ex. You stop carrying old fights into new connections. Your nervous system gets a break. Your heart gets a fresh start.

Mindful Minute—The Empty Chair Technique
A tool from Gestalt therapy, this is a powerful and practical way to *release* old pain and reconnect with your emotional truth. At first glance, it might seem simple (and silly)—even a little strange—but don't underestimate its impact.

You sit across from an empty chair and imagine someone from your past sitting in it—maybe a parent, an ex, or even a version of *you* at a younger age. Then, you say out loud what you *wish* you could have said. The feelings you never expressed. The boundaries you needed. The apologies you never got. The hurt you've been carrying.

Why is this so healing?

Instead of bottling up unspoken needs or fears to avoid conflict or abandonment, you can finally express them freely and without judgment. Speaking these truths aloud helps your brain process and release old emotional pain, shifting you from simply reliving the hurt to taking control of it. Most importantly, it offers a sense of closure that doesn't rely on the other person, allowing you to find healing and peace on your terms.

The Power of Forgiveness in Healing Attachment Wounds

Forgiveness doesn't mean forgetting or pretending the pain didn't happen, excusing hurtful behavior, or letting someone back into your life. What it *does* mean is choosing to release the emotional weight that's been holding you back. Especially for those with anxious attachment, forgiveness can be a deeply healing act—one that breaks cycles of pain and softens the grip of old wounds.

People with anxious attachment often carry unresolved hurt from early relationships where love felt inconsistent, conditional, or unsafe. This pain can echo into adult relationships, creating fear, overdependence, or emotional reactivity. According to Enright and Fitzgibbons (2000), forgiveness allows individuals to move beyond trauma and reclaim their emotional well-being. It shifts the power dynamic—you're no longer defined by what happened to you but by how you choose to respond to it.

Forgiveness is less about the other person and more about *you*. It's a radical act of self-care. It allows you to release resentment, regret, or unanswered questions. And when that emotional load is lifted, something powerful happens: you create space for trust, safety, and genuine connection.

Forgiveness can be the turning point in healing attachment wounds. It helps regulate your emotions, lowers anxiety, and allows you to show up in relationships with more clarity and self-compassion. It's not easy, and it often takes time, but the freedom it brings is worth it. You don't have to carry the past forever. You're allowed to heal. Remember that forgiveness is the boundary between your past and your healing.

Creating New Emotional Narratives
One of the most powerful aspects of healing anxious attachment is realizing that the stories you tell yourself are not fixed truths—they're *narratives*, and narratives can be rewritten. According to Narrative Therapy (White & Epston, 1990), we all live through the lens of the stories we've absorbed and internalized over time. For those with anxious attachment, those stories often sound like: *"I'm too needy," "I always get left behind,"* or *"If I don't prove my worth, I'll lose them."*

These narratives didn't come from anywhere. They usually begin in childhood, shaped by inconsistent caregiving or early experiences where love felt unpredictable or conditional. Over time, these beliefs become internalized, repeating like background noise in your relationships. And without realizing it, you start living in a story that says you're too much, or not enough, or somehow responsible for being left.

But here's the truth: *those are old stories, not your destiny.* Narrative therapy encourages you to challenge these beliefs, look at the bigger picture of who you are, and begin authoring a new story grounded in self-worth, agency, and emotional safety.

This might sound like: *"I'm learning to be secure," "I'm not too much—I just have deep needs,"* or *"I can be loved for who I am."* When you tell yourself a different story, you start to *live* differently, too. You're no longer stuck in the past—you're actively creating a new emotional reality, one chapter at a time.

Reframing With Truth
Here are statements to help us reframe the narrative that can make us doubt and question ourselves.

- I wasn't clingy—I was craving connection in a space that felt uncertain."

- "Their inability to love me consistently wasn't a reflection of my worth."

- "I don't have to earn love by overgiving or shrinking myself."

- "It's safe for me to ask for reassurance. My needs are valid."

- "I am not broken—I'm healing from experiences that taught me to fear love."

- "Needing closeness doesn't make me needy—it makes me human."

- "I can be loved without performing or proving my value."

- "My emotions aren't too much—they're information, not a burden."

- "I no longer have to chase people to feel secure. I can offer that to myself."

- "It wasn't that I was unlovable—I loved people who couldn't meet me where I was."

You Deserve Self-Compassion

Self-compassion isn't just a nice idea—it's a transformational (and continual) practice. For individuals with anxious attachment, it serves as a tool for healing from the inside out. For so long, you may have been taught to view love as something you had to *earn*, to see your value through the lens of other people's approval. You may have believed that your worth depended on meeting the needs of others, being perfect, or managing every relationship with an anxious, hypervigilant energy. The truth is that self-compassion liberates you from that exhausting cycle.

When you learn to be kind to yourself—especially when you feel insecure, overwhelmed, or afraid—you stop outsourcing your worth to others. You stop seeking validation outside of yourself and cultivate an inner foundation of love, acceptance, and peace. This doesn't mean you stop seeking connection or love from others, but you no longer tie your sense of self to their approval or emotional availability. You begin to embody the love you've been desperately chasing.

Healing anxious attachment means letting go of the old, deep-seated belief that you must be flawless or constantly available to be worthy of love. Self-compassion teaches you that imperfection is not something to hide but to embrace. When you're able to be kind to yourself in moments of pain, fear, or doubt, you teach your nervous system to feel safe *in your presence*. You're no longer running from your emotions or stuffing them down; you're giving them space to be processed and integrated without judgment.

And here's the most beautiful part of it: You're not here to be perfect. You're not here to mold yourself into someone you think others want you to be. You're here to be you—messy, emotional, evolving, and *real*. You are allowed to be imperfect, make mistakes, struggle, and rise again. Your humanity is what makes you relatable, lovable, and valuable.

The version of you who is raw, vulnerable, and genuine? They're already worthy of love. No conditions. No strings attached. You don't have to change to be deserving. Love isn't something you have to chase—it's something you can offer yourself and others simply by being true to yourself. This is where healing begins: in accepting yourself, flaws and all. When you start to hold yourself with compassion and kindness, you shift how you present yourself in the world. You don't need to prove your worth. It's inherent in your being.

When you choose self-compassion, you shift from a place of anxiety and self-doubt to one of inner peace and security. You create a life where love is no longer something you have to chase but something you experience because you've given it to yourself first. You stop trying to win others over by being perfect and start attracting connections based on authenticity, vulnerability, and shared humanity.

Ultimately, self-compassion is the most valuable gift you can give yourself. It's not just a tool for coping—it's the key to transforming your inner world. When you embrace yourself fully, flaws and all, you begin to heal the foundation of your relationships, starting with the one you have with yourself.

Quiz Time—How Compassionate Are You With Yourself?

Reflect on your behavior and inner dialogue during moments of stress or disappointment. Rate each statement from 1 (never) to 5 (always). Tally your score at the end of the quiz.

1. When I make a mistake, I criticize myself harshly.

2. I allow myself to feel upset without trying to push the emotions away.

3. I offer myself kind words or affirmations when struggling emotionally.

4. I compare myself negatively to others when I feel down.

5. I practice patience and understanding with myself when things don't go as planned.

6. I feel guilty or ashamed when I take time for self-care or rest.

7. I regularly remind myself that I am doing the best I can in difficult situations.

8. I find it hard to forgive myself when I've hurt someone or made a mistake.

9. I talk to myself like a good friend who is struggling.

10. I embrace my flaws and imperfections without judgment.

Analyzing Your Results

10-20: You may struggle with self-compassion and often criticize or neglect yourself when faced with challenges. Begin practicing small acts of kindness toward yourself.

21-35: You are developing self-compassion but may still face moments of self-criticism. Continue nurturing self-love and offering yourself the same understanding you would give a friend.

36-50: You likely have a good foundation of self-compassion and can support yourself emotionally during tough times. Keep building on this practice, and continue being kind to yourself.

Quiz Time—Self-Love and Emotional Health

How do you treat yourself emotionally? Are you kind, or are you harsh? Rate each statement from 1 (strongly disagree) to 5 (strongly agree). Tally your score at the end.

1. I prioritize my emotional needs, even when it feels challenging.

2. I set healthy boundaries to protect my emotional well-being.

3. I feel comfortable saying "no" to things that drain me emotionally.

4. I make time for activities that nourish and restore me, even during busy periods.

5. I trust myself to make decisions in my best interest.

6. I take time to recognize and celebrate my strengths and accomplishments.

7. I can forgive myself when I make mistakes without harsh self-judgment.

8. I practice gratitude for my progress in my healing journey.

9. I deserve love and care, even when I'm imperfect.

10. I allow myself to experience joy, even in challenging times.

Analyzing Your Results

10-20: You may struggle to prioritize your emotional needs and self-acceptance. Start by setting small, achievable goals to practice self-love and emotional care.

21-35: You are on your way to building a stronger emotional foundation but may still find it hard to embrace self-love in certain situations fully.

36-50: You likely have a strong sense of self-love and prioritize your emotional well-being. Continue to nurture this practice, and don't hesitate to support others in their emotional growth.

Remember—You are worthy. You are enough. You have always been enough.

Chapter 7:
BUILDING SECURE AND LASTING RELATIONSHIPS

A secure relationship is not about never being triggered—it's about knowing you can come back to safety, together.

–Dr. Stan Tatkin

D o you know what a healthy relationship looks like? A healthy, secure relationship is one with mutual trust, open communication, and emotional support between both individuals. Partners feel safe to express their thoughts and feelings without fear of judgment or rejection. They respect each other's boundaries and work together to navigate challenges. This chapter will explore how individuals with anxious attachment styles can enter and nurture such relationships by choosing compatible partners, practicing secure attachment behaviors, and creating a shared vision for love.

Choosing the Right Partner

Did you know that knowing what a healthy relationship is is one thing, but finding a partner who will nurture and develop these qualities is another?

The Attachment Theory suggests that the relationships we form early on shape how we love as adults (Hazan & Shaver, 2017). When you struggle with anxious attachments, it's important to choose an emotionally responsive and consistent partner, which can help you feel secure.

In contrast, choosing someone who is dismissive, emotionally unavailable, or inconsistent may reinforce feelings of fear and uncertainty. A partner who validates your emotions listens to your needs and demonstrates a willingness to nurture the relationship can help you break free from the cycle of anxiety. Research indicates that secure partners encourage positive attachment behaviors and help create a balanced, safe relationship environment (Johnson, 2004). The right partner doesn't just ease the fear of abandonment—they help you heal and grow into a more secure version of yourself

Red Flags vs. Green Flags in a Partner

When finding a suitable and compatible partner, it is important to pay attention to the little things—the behaviors and actions that show whether a person is genuinely a good fit for you. Certain signs, such as respect, kindness, and open communication, indicate that a relationship can be healthy and supportive.

Certain red flags—such as dishonesty or a lack of empathy—can signal potential relationship problems. Recognizing these signs early on can help build stronger, healthier relationships, or it can be a sign not to pursue the person.

Red Flags

- **Inconsistent communication:** If your partner frequently fails to communicate or sends mixed signals, it can increase feelings of anxiety and insecurity. This unpredictability often leaves you unsure of where you stand, making it harder to build trust.

- **Avoidance of emotional intimacy:** When someone is reluctant to share their feelings or engage in meaningful emotional exchanges, it can be a sign of difficulty forming deep, lasting connections. Emotional intimacy is a cornerstone of healthy relationships; without it, the bond can feel shallow.

- **Disrespect for boundaries:** Partners who consistently ignore or disregard your boundaries create an unsafe environment. This can lead to feelings of discomfort or violation, which slowly erode trust and security in the relationship.

- **Lack of accountability:** If your partner deflects responsibility for their actions or blames others for their mistakes, it creates an imbalance in the relationship. This behavior prevents growth and fosters an unpredictable, unstable dynamic, leaving you with little assurance of reliability.

- **Jealousy and control:** Excessive jealousy or attempts to control your actions, friendships, or independence are major red flags. These behaviors stem from insecurity and can lead to a toxic relationship environment.

- **Gaslighting:** If your partner makes you doubt your reality or denies things they've said or done, it's a serious red flag. Gaslighting is a form of manipulation that can erode your confidence and sense of self.

Green Flags

Green flags in a relationship are just as important as spotting red flags. Green flags are positive behaviors that indicate a partner is emotionally mature, reliable, and aligned with your values.

These signs tell you the relationship has a strong foundation built on trust, respect, and mutual care.

- **Consistent and open communication:** A partner who engages in regular, honest dialogue fosters trust and understanding. When your partner consistently checks in, listens actively, and expresses themselves openly, it creates a safe environment for both individuals to share their feelings, fears, and needs. Healthy communication strengthens the emotional connection and helps prevent misunderstandings from escalating.

Example: If you're upset, your partner listens without interrupting, and when it's your turn to listen, they make sure they understand your perspective. They don't dismiss your feelings and try to resolve issues together.

- **Emotional availability:** The willingness to share feelings and support each other's emotional needs strengthens the bond. Emotional availability means being open to discussing not just the good parts of life but also the challenges, fears, and vulnerabilities. An emotionally available partner will validate your emotions and create a safe space to express yourself without fear of judgment.

Example: After a hard day, your partner doesn't just talk about themselves; they ask how you feel and offer emotional support. They don't shy away from tough conversations, and they express empathy when you need it most.

- **Respect for boundaries:** Acknowledging and honoring personal limits ensures both partners feel valued and safe. Boundaries are vital in any relationship, as they help both people maintain their individuality and prevent unhealthy enmeshment. A partner who respects boundaries listens when you express your needs and makes adjustments to ensure your emotional and physical comfort.

Example: If you need space to recharge or ask for certain behaviors to be avoided, your partner listens without taking it personally. They understand that healthy boundaries lead to a stronger connection.

- **Accountability and growth:** Taking responsibility for actions and committing to personal development contribute to a healthy relationship dynamic. A partner who acknowledges their mistakes, learns from them, and strives to improve builds a relationship based on mutual respect and trust. This willingness to improve strengthens the foundation of the relationship, ensuring that both people can grow together.

Example: If a conflict arises, your partner doesn't shy away from admitting their part in the situation. They express a sincere desire to change or apologize, showing growth and effort in becoming a better partner.

- **Mutual support and encouragement:** Healthy relationships are built on mutual respect and encouragement. A partner who supports your dreams, goals, and personal growth without fear or jealousy is a true ally in your life. This dynamic creates an environment where both individuals feel safe pursuing their ambitions and are motivated to succeed.

Example: Your partner actively encourages you to chase your dreams, whether it's pursuing a new career, learning a new skill, or taking on a personal project. They celebrate your successes without comparing or undermining them.

- **Shared values and goals:** The alignment of important life values and future goals creates a strong foundation for long-term compatibility. While differences can exist, shared values around family, career ambitions, and lifestyle preferences are essential to maintaining harmony in the relationship.

Example: You and your partner prioritize open communication, kindness, and honesty. Whether discussing family dynamics or future plans, your values align, and you work toward similar goals.

- **Mutual respect for independence:** A partner who values and encourages your individuality is a green flag. It shows they understand the importance of personal space and the relationship. You can be your true self, pursue hobbies, and spend time apart without feeling guilty or neglected.

Example: Your partner encourages you to hang out with friends, pursue your personal interests, and maintain your own identity while still fostering intimacy. They appreciate that you have your own life outside of the relationship.

These positive behaviors help reduce anxiety and insecurity, laying the groundwork for a long-lasting, fulfilling partnership. Recognizing green flags in a relationship can allow you to fully invest in building a deep and meaningful connection with a partner who shares your emotional capacity and commitment.

How to Recognize Emotionally Available Partners

Finding and establishing a healthy and secure relationship with emotional availability will be key to having a relationship that won't trigger your anxieties and stresses. One reason is that emotionally available individuals are attuned to their own emotions and able to understand and empathize with the emotions of others, especially their partner. These individuals can create a nurturing environment by offering emotional support and validation, helping their partner feel heard, understood, and valued. Recognizing emotional availability in a partner is essential for building a strong, resilient relationship founded on trust, mutual respect, and emotional safety (Bowlby, 1969).

One of the most telling traits of an emotionally available partner is their ability to demonstrate empathy. They don't just listen—they strive to understand and respond to the emotions that are expressed. This ability to empathize shows they are invested in the relationship and their partner's emotional experience. According to Dr. John Gottman (2018), couples who engage in empathetic listening tend to have better outcomes in relationships, as they can work through conflicts and emotional challenges more easily than couples who lack empathy. For instance, when you are upset, an emotionally available partner will seek to understand and validate your feelings rather than dismiss or minimize your experience.

Along with empathy, emotionally available partners tend to be better at active listening. To be an active listener, you must be fully engaged with what the other person is saying—acknowledging their feelings, asking clarifying questions, and being present. This form of communication builds intimacy, as both partners can feel seen and heard.

Dr. Sue Johnson, a leading expert on emotionally focused therapy, emphasizes that emotional responsiveness and engagement are fundamental to forming emotional bonds (Johnson, 2004). Emotionally available partners take the time to listen and engage with their partner's emotional world, ensuring that both parties feel connected.

Furthermore, emotionally available individuals are comfortable with intimacy and vulnerability. They do not shy away from sharing their feelings and experiences, allowing their partner to do the same. This openness creates a safe space for emotional sharing, which is essential for building trust and closeness.

Emotional availability is also linked to a willingness to invest time and effort into the relationship's growth. Emotionally available partners will actively nurture the relationship, engage in problem-solving, and work together to overcome challenges (Mikulincer & Shaver, 2007).

Avoiding Anxious-Avoidant Relationships

In relationships, people with anxious attachment styles and those with avoidant attachment styles often find themselves drawn to each other. Still, this connection can create a cycle of frustration and emotional distance. To understand this better, let's examine what each attachment style means and how they interact.

People with an anxious attachment style usually seek closeness, approval, and reassurance from their partners. They may have a deep-seated fear of abandonment or worry that they are not loved enough. According to Bowlby (1969), the founder of attachment theory, these individuals often need constant reassurance and validation from their partner, as they have learned to seek security through emotional closeness. However, this can lead to feelings of insecurity in the relationship, which can drive the anxious individual to demand more attention and closeness.

In contrast, individuals with an avoidant attachment style tend to value independence and self-sufficiency. They are often uncomfortable with emotional closeness or relying on others. Bartholomew and Horowitz (1991) explain that avoidantly attached individuals might push their partners away when they feel their autonomy is threatened. The fear of being controlled or losing their independence often leads them to distance themselves emotionally, even if they still care about their partner.

This dynamic of pursuit and withdrawal can create tension. The anxiously attached person feels rejected or neglected when their partner withdraws, intensifying their need for reassurance and closeness. This heightened demand for intimacy can, in turn, make the avoidant partner feel overwhelmed and suffocated, which only leads to further withdrawal. This cycle of emotional demand and emotional retreat often results in dissatisfaction and frustration for both partners.

Psychologist John Bowlby (1969), who developed attachment theory, suggests that our attachment behaviors are rooted in early relationships, particularly with caregivers, and these patterns often carry over into adult romantic relationships. Sue Johnson (2004), a leading researcher in attachment-based couples therapy, notes that these patterns can become destructive over time, leading couples to feel stuck in a cycle where one partner's anxiety increases the other's avoidance and vice versa.

Recognizing this pattern is the first step in breaking the cycle. Understanding how attachment styles influence behavior can help individuals make more informed relationship decisions. Mikulincer and Shaver (2010) argue that understanding one's attachment style—and how it aligns with a partner—can empower individuals to build healthier, more secure connections.

In therapy, learning to communicate effectively and understand your and your partner's attachment needs can help break these destructive cycles. Research by Johnson (2004) indicates that couples who work together to understand and address their attachment dynamics can foster more secure and emotionally fulfilling relationships.

By learning about these patterns and making conscious efforts to change, individuals can develop healthier relationships that respect both partners' needs for intimacy and independence.

What Secure Attachment Looks Like in Daily Life
Secure attachment in relationships is like the glue that holds everything together. Securely attached individuals know how to communicate openly, share their feelings, and listen to their partner with empathy. They're not afraid to express their needs but also respect their partner's emotional space. It's about finding a balance between being close and giving each other room to grow as individuals.

This balance fosters trust, safety, and a deep emotional connection, which are the foundation of a healthy relationship. For example, if one person is feeling down, the securely attached partner is there to offer comfort, but without overwhelming them. Instead of clinging or pulling away, they're responsive to their partner's emotional state, ready to communicate and work through difficulties together. This openness and mutual respect create a supportive environment for the relationship.

Rewriting Relationship Patterns With Intention

For those with an anxious attachment style, it might feel like their past patterns of seeking reassurance or fearing abandonment will never change. However, these patterns can be rewritten with conscious effort and self-awareness. The first step is recognizing these behaviors—maybe you tend to chase after your partner when they pull away, or you struggle with self-doubt in relationships. The next step is challenging the beliefs that fuel them. For instance, the belief that "If I'm not constantly available or perfect, I'll lose my partner" can be examined and replaced with healthier thoughts, such as "I am worthy of love and respect, even if I take time for myself."

One effective way to manage anxious attachment behaviors is practicing self-soothing techniques, like deep breathing, journaling, or mindfulness, to calm anxiety during moments of stress. Engaging in therapy or support groups can provide additional guidance in building healthier relational patterns. Slowly but surely, the more you embrace secure behaviors—such as communicating openly, setting boundaries, and not reacting impulsively—the more these behaviors will become second nature, leading to more fulfilling, balanced relationships.

The Importance of Patience in Relationship Growth
Building a secure relationship doesn't happen overnight, especially when you've been used to anxious attachment patterns. It's a growth journey that requires patience with both yourself and your partner. Change takes time, and it's important to be compassionate with yourself when setbacks occur. For example, maybe there's a moment when old habits sneak in, and you feel that familiar wave of insecurity or fear of abandonment. Instead of criticizing yourself for not being "perfect," acknowledge that progress is gradual.

Recognizing that these moments are part of the healing process can help maintain motivation to keep moving forward. By accepting that there will be ups and downs and allowing yourself and your partner the space to grow, you can stay committed to building a stronger, more secure relationship over time. The key is to focus on progress, not perfection, and celebrate the small steps toward healthier emotional patterns.

Practicing Secure Attachment Behaviors
It is not always easy to transition from anxious to secure, but there are a few things you can do to improve and establish secure attachment behaviors.

- **Open and honest communication:** Share your feelings, needs, and thoughts with your partner openly. Securely attached individuals are not afraid to express themselves and communicate calmly, even when discussing complex topics. For example, instead of bottling up frustration, you might say, "I've been feeling a little disconnected lately, and I want to talk about it."

- **Active listening:** Pay attention and be fully present when your partner shares their emotions or thoughts. Active listening involves hearing what they say and validating their feelings. For example, instead of interrupting, you might say, "I hear you, and I understand that this situation is stressful for you."

- **Comforting and calming your partner:** When your partner is upset or stressed, offer comfort without trying to fix everything immediately. Secure attachment means being a source of emotional support while respecting your partner's space. For example, gently holding their hand and saying, "I'm here for you, and I'll support you through this," can provide a sense of safety.

- **Respecting personal boundaries:** Recognize and respect your partner's need for space or independence. Securely attached individuals understand that healthy relationships balance togetherness and autonomy. For example, if your partner needs time alone to recharge, instead of feeling abandoned, you can say, "I respect that you need some space right now. I'll be here when you're ready."

- **Self-regulation during conflict:** Instead of escalating or withdrawing, practice staying calm and regulated during disagreements. Secure attachment involves healthily managing your emotions. For example, if you're feeling overwhelmed during a conversation, you might say, "I'm feeling really upset right now, so I'm going to take a short break and come back to this when I'm calmer."

- **Balancing dependence and independence:** Secure attachment involves balancing the need for closeness and maintaining your sense of independence. You can depend on your partner while also maintaining your sense of self and pursuing your own hobbies, friendships, and goals. For example, you might say, "I love spending time with you, but I also need time to focus on my interests. Both are important to me."

- **Offering reassurance and affirmation:** Securely attached individuals offer reassurance when their partner feels insecure without being overbearing. For example, when your partner is anxious, you might say, "I'm here for you, and we're in this together. You're not alone in this."

- **Setting and respecting boundaries:** Setting boundaries around what is acceptable and respecting each other's limits is a sign of secure attachment. For example, you might say, "It's important that we have some quiet time at night to unwind. I'd love it if we could both respect that time."

- **Forgiving and moving forward:** In secure relationships, conflicts and mistakes don't lead to long-term resentment. Securely attached individuals can forgive their partner's missteps and work together to improve the relationship. For example, you might say, "I understand that you didn't mean to hurt me. Let's talk about it and move forward."

- **Celebrating each other's achievements:** Securely attached partners celebrate each other's successes without feeling threatened or jealous. For example, when your partner accomplishes something, you might say, "I'm so proud of you! Your hard work is paying off, and I love seeing you thrive."

Creating a Vision for Love

Do you know what kind of relationship you want or deserve? Knowing what you want will help you create healthy and safe boundaries for potential relationships. Romantic relationships aren't just about love—it's about the kind of partnership that feels right for you.

Do you want to feel a deep sense of emotional intimacy, engage in good communication, and openly share your dreams and goals?

Consider the qualities that are important to you—things like respect, support, and trust—and imagine a relationship that ticks those boxes. Knowing what you want can guide your choices, helping you build a partnership that aligns with your heart's desires (Hazan & Shaver, 2017).

Aligning Your Values With Your Relationship Goals

To create a lasting, fulfilling relationship, you want to find a partner whose values align with your relationship goals. For example, if you value independence but also want a close connection, discussing how both partners can honor that balance is crucial. Conversations about your goals, boundaries, and expectations help prevent misunderstandings and ensure you're both on the same page. When your values are in sync, it strengthens your foundation and makes it easier to navigate life's challenges together (Bowlby, 1969).

Not only is having similar or aligned values important, but having emotional security with this person can also be beneficial. Think of it as tending a garden—communication, respect, and mutual appreciation are essential.

Remember that love is not just found but built through intentional actions and emotional investment. By choosing a partner who is compatible with your needs and wants, practicing secure attachment behaviors, and creating a shared vision for love, individuals can cultivate fulfilling and enduring relationships.

Activity—Creating a Relationship Vision Board

Visualizing the desired relationship can be powerful in manifesting one's goals.

Creating a vision board with images, quotes, and symbols that represent the qualities and dynamics of the ideal relationship can serve as a daily reminder and motivator.

This practice can help clarify intentions and inspire actions toward building a secure and lasting partnership.

Quiz Time—Are You Building Secure and Lasting Relationships

Answer the following questions based on your current or most recent romantic relationship or typical relationship patterns.

For each question, choose the response that feels most true for you.

Tally your responses at the end.

1. When your partner doesn't respond to a text right away, how do you usually feel?
A. Calm—I assume they're just busy.
B. A little worried, but I try to distract myself.
C. Anxious and panicked—I wonder if they're upset or losing interest.

2. How do you tend to choose partners?
   A. I look for emotional availability and consistency.
   B. I often go for the spark and chemistry, even if they're emotionally distant.
   C. I'm not sure—I often end up in confusing or hot-cold relationships.

3. When there's a disagreement, how do you typically respond?
   A. I try to talk things through calmly and listen actively.
   B. I feel overwhelmed and either shut down or chase after them.
   C. I fear they'll leave, so I try to fix it quickly— even if I'm not in the wrong.

4. How comfortable are you expressing your needs in a relationship?
   A. Very comfortable—it feels normal and healthy.
   B. Somewhat comfortable, but I often worry I'll seem "too much."
   C. Not comfortable at all—I often suppress my needs to keep the peace.

5. What qualities do you look for in a partner?
   A. Kindness, emotional availability, and shared values.
   B. Passion, excitement, and intensity.
   C. I'm not sure—I hope they don't leave.

Rate yourself on a scale from 1 (Never True) to 5 (Always True)

6. I feel safe and secure in my close relationships.

7. I trust my partner to show up emotionally. I can set and maintain healthy boundaries.

8. I choose partners who make me feel seen, heard, and valued.

9. I believe I deserve a stable, lasting, loving relationship.

Analyzing Your Results
Mostly A's:

You're developing or have built a secure base for healthy relationships. You choose emotionally available partners and tend to manage attachment fears well. Keep nurturing those habits!

Mostly B's:

You're becoming aware of your patterns but might still fall into familiar anxious loops. Continue focusing on self-regulation, communication, and choosing emotionally safe partners.

Mostly C's:

You may still be operating from old attachment wounds. This is a sign to go deeper into healing—practice self-compassion, build inner safety, and clarify your relationship vision.

Call to Action—Relationship Journal Prompts

Self-awareness and reflection are not always easy when it comes to understanding and recognizing the type of love we want.

Here are three journal prompts to help you understand what you want in your relationship, whether romantic or not.

- What patterns in your relationships do you want to shift?

- What are three qualities of a partner that make you feel emotionally safe?

- How will you start showing up as a secure partner to yourself?

Conclusion
YOUR NEW
CHAPTER BEGINS

*With self-compassion, we give ourselves
the same kindness and care we'd give to
a good friend.*

–Kristin Neff

A s you venture into this new journey with greater understanding and the realization and recognition that healing is possible, taking a moment of grace for yourself is important. Look forward with hope and empowerment. Relationships are complicated, and there are influences often beyond our control; however, when we can take the time to reflect and see how our past and relationships have impacted our present and future, we can work towards transforming ourselves into a secure, happier, and more fulfilled person.

Throughout the chapters, we have covered and discussed:

- **Self-awareness:** Understanding your attachment style allows you to identify relationship triggers and responses, which is critical for change.

- **Self-regulation:** Developing emotional regulation techniques helps manage anxiety and fosters a sense of inner peace, reducing the impact of external relationship dynamics.

- **Building secure connections:** Engaging in relationships with partners who exhibit secure attachment behaviors provides a model for healthy interactions and supports your growth.

- **Therapeutic interventions:** Seeking professional help, such as therapy, can provide personalized strategies and support, facilitating more profound healing and understanding.

- **Creating a vision for love:** Defining what a healthy relationship looks like for you and aligning your actions with this vision guides you toward fulfilling partnerships.

Lasting Change Comes Through Never Giving Up

While understanding the theories and strategies is a crucial first step, the actual transformation occurs when these insights are applied daily. Implementing learned strategies requires commitment, self-compassion, and consistent effort.

While we have covered various concepts, the following actionable practices will truly make a positive and beneficial difference in your life.

Daily Self-Reflection

Allocating a few minutes daily for self-reflection can significantly enhance self-awareness and emotional intelligence. This practice involves examining your thoughts, feelings, and behaviors to gain deeper insight into your emotional landscape.

Benefits:

- **Enhanced self-awareness:** Regular reflection helps identify emotional triggers and patterns, facilitating personal growth.

- **Stress reduction:** Expressing thoughts and feelings through writing can alleviate stress and promote emotional well-being.

Actioning This:

- **Consistency:** Dedicate a specific time each day for journaling to build a sustainable habit.

- **Authenticity:** Write honestly about your experiences without judgment to fully benefit from the practice.

- **Gratitude practice:** Incorporate noting things you're grateful for to foster a positive mindset.

Practice Self-Compassion

Treating yourself with kindness, especially during challenging times, is fundamental to healing anxious attachment. Self-compassion involves recognizing your inherent worth and extending the same care to yourself that you offer to others.

Benefits:

- **Improved emotional well-being:** Self-compassion reduces negative self-talk and promotes a positive self-image.

- **Resilience building:** Being compassionate with yourself enhances your ability to cope with life's challenges.

Actioning This:

- **Mindful awareness:** Observe your thoughts and feelings without judgment, acknowledging them as part of your human experience.

- **Positive affirmations:** Challenge negative beliefs by replacing them with affirmations of your strengths and achievements.

- **Self-forgiveness:** Release guilt and regret by understanding that making mistakes is a natural part of growth.

Seek Support

Building a supportive network is crucial for healing and growth. Connecting with individuals who encourage your development and provide a safe space for vulnerability can significantly impact your journey toward secure attachment.

Benefits:
- **Emotional validation:** Sharing experiences with empathetic listeners can help affirm your feelings and reduce isolation.

- **Perspective expansion:** Supportive relationships offer diverse viewpoints, facilitating personal insight and problem-solving.

Actioning This:
- **Identify supportive individuals:** Engage with friends, family members, or support groups that foster a nurturing environment.

- **Communicate needs:** Clearly express your desire for support and specify how others can assist you effectively.

- **Reciprocity:** Offer support to others, creating a mutual exchange that strengthens bonds and reinforces your support system.

Set Boundaries
Establishing healthy boundaries is essential for protecting your emotional well-being and fostering respectful relationships. Boundaries define acceptable behaviors and ensure that your needs are honored.

Benefits:
- **Enhanced self-respect:** Clear boundaries reinforce your self-worth and prevent feelings of resentment.

- **Improved relationships:** Respecting boundaries leads to more balanced and fulfilling interactions.

Actioning This:
- **Self-identification:** Reflect on your values and limits to understand where boundaries are needed.

- **Clear communication:** Articulate your boundaries assertively and respectfully to others.

- **Consistent enforcement:** Maintain your boundaries to reinforce their importance and ensure mutual respect.

Pursue Professional Help if Needed

If past traumas or deeply ingrained patterns are hindering your progress, seeking professional assistance is vital to healing. Therapists specializing in attachment issues can provide tailored strategies and support.

Benefits:
- **Expert guidance:** Professionals offer evidence-based interventions suited to your unique situation.

- **Safe exploration:** Therapy offers a confidential space to explore sensitive topics and emotions.

Actioning This:
- **Research professionals:** Look for therapists with experience in attachment theory and a therapeutic approach that resonates with you.

- **Commit to the process:** Engage actively in therapy, set goals, and be open to the journey of self-discovery.

- **Utilize resources:** Incorporate tools and exercises your therapist provides into your daily routine to reinforce progress.

Embrace Your Worthiness of Secure Love and Positivity

As you incorporate these strategies into your life, it cannot be stressed enough that healing is a journey, not a destination. Each step, no matter how small, brings you closer to the secure, nurturing relationships you deeply deserve. Embrace your inherent worthiness and approach this journey with patience, self-compassion, and a sense of grace.

Reflecting on Maya Angelou's words, *"You alone are enough. You have nothing to prove to anybody"* (Angelou, n.d.) allows you to internalize your value and move forward with confidence. You do not need to earn love through perfection, performance, or people-pleasing.

Your commitment to change and growth is a testament to your strength and resilience. You are no longer just surviving love—you are learning how to thrive in it.

Believe in your capacity to heal, grow, and attract the kind of love that honors your heart. Your past does not define you. Your daily choices, your self-awareness, and your courage to show up for yourself—those are what shape your future.

Step into this new chapter with hope, determination, and the unwavering belief that you are—and have always been—worthy of secure, lasting love.

You have everything within you to create the life and relationships you deserve. Trust yourself, embrace the process, and celebrate your growth.

21 DAY ACTION PLAN

Congratulations on making it through the book.

Remember that you can refer to specific chapters at any time, redo the quizzes, or answer the prompts again. As you navigate through life, you may encounter new territories and situations that trigger your anxiety more than others—it's okay.

Short on time? Unsure which chapter you need?

Here is a quick guide on healing from anxious attachments in 21 days.

Week 1: Understanding Yourself (Days 1–7)
Goal: Build awareness of your thoughts, triggers, and patterns
Linked to Chapters 1 to 4

Day 1: Identify Your Overthinking Patterns

- Journal: What situations trigger spiraling thoughts?

- Write one recurring worry and how often it comes up.

Day 2: Name the Fear of Abandonment

- Reflect: What does being abandoned mean to you?

- Write about your earliest memory of this fear.

Day 3: Trace the Origin

- Explore: Did a caregiver, friend, or ex contribute to this fear?

- Acknowledge that the past isn't your fault—but the healing is your responsibility.

Day 4: Meet Your Inner Critic

- Notice the negative self-talk you engage in.

- Give it a name (e.g., "Doubt Debbie") to separate it from your true self.

Day 5: Learn About Attachment Styles

- Take a quiz to discover your style (anxious, avoidant, secure, etc.).

- Journal: How does this show up in your relationships?

Day 6: Practice Mindful Awareness

- Set a timer and do five minutes of deep breathing or grounding.

- Write down what you notice when you slow down.

Day 7: Self-Compassion Check-In

- Write yourself a compassionate letter.

- Say: "I'm learning. I'm allowed to be human. I'm worthy of love."

Week 2: Challenging and Rewriting Patterns (Days 8–14)
Goal: Change the mental and emotional habits that hurt your relationships
Linked to Chapters 5–7

Day 8: Pause the Spiral

- When a worry hits, write it down and say: "This is a thought, not a fact."

- Use a five-minute distraction technique (walk, music, puzzle).

Day 9: Reframe the Narrative

- Take one fear and flip it: *"They'll leave me"* → *"If they stay, it's because they want to."*

Day 10: Boundaries Are Bridges

- List where you overgive or overshare to feel safe.

- Pick one boundary to practice this week.

Day 11: Communicate From the Heart

- Use "I" statements: *"I feel anxious when I don't hear back. Can we talk about how we check in?"*

Day 12: Build Secure Habits

- Ask yourself: "What would a securely attached person do?"

- Do that thing—whether it's texting calmly or giving space.

Day 13: Inner Child Soothing

- Talk to your younger self: *"You're not alone anymore. I've got you now."*

Day 14: Celebrate Small Wins

- Write down three things you handled differently this week.

- Acknowledge your growth, no matter how small.

Week 3: Building Lasting Love (Days 15–21)
Goal: Create connection and confidence in your relationships
Linked to Chapters 8–10

Day 15: Clarify Your Relationship Vision

- What does a healthy relationship look like to you?

- Write down your top three values in love.

Day 16: Recognize Real Red Flags vs. Fear

- Make two columns: Red flags vs. Anxious Triggers

- Learn to tell the difference.

Day 17: Practice Secure Responses

- Next time you feel triggered, pause, breathe, and respond instead of reacting.

- Write about how it felt to choose calm.

Day 18: Foster Emotional Safety

- Ask: "How can I make this relationship safer for both of us?"

- Try active listening or expressing appreciation.

Day 19: Invite Vulnerability

- Share one fear or truth with someone you trust.

- Practice being open without expecting perfection.

Day 20: Build Interdependence, Not Dependence

- List what makes *you* whole outside of your partner.

- Commit to one activity that brings you joy and confidence.

Day 21: Commit to Growth

- Write a self-promise: *"I choose connection over fear. I trust myself. I deserve safe love."*

- Create a plan to check in weekly with yourself from now on.

Remember

You've just completed 21 powerful days of showing up for yourself, healing, and future relationships. That's something to be proud of.

Over the past three weeks, you've uncovered your attachment patterns, practiced self-compassion, learned how to communicate your needs, and built tools to calm anxiety before it takes over. You've also learned that anxious attachment isn't a flaw—it's a survival response from your past. But with awareness, intention, and kindness, you've started rewriting the story.

Truthfully, healing isn't about never feeling anxious again—it's about responding differently when you do. You now have strategies to pause, reflect, and connect without fear.

Keep practicing, keep showing up. You're building new emotional muscles, and like any growth, it takes time.

Most importantly, remember this: you are not too much. You are not broken. You are worthy of love that feels safe, steady, and real.

Let this be your reminder: secure love doesn't start with someone else but with how you love yourself.

The journey doesn't end here. This is just your beginning.

A Heartfelt Thank You & Your Journey Continues

Dear Reader,

Thank you for choosing **The Complete Roadmap to Healing Anxious Attachment**. Guiding you toward secure, joyful love was an honor. You've taken a crucial step; keep nurturing your inner peace and believing in your worth.

Your Voice Matters: Please Leave a Review on Amazon!

If this book helped you, please share your experience. Your honest review is incredibly powerful:

- Help others find their roadmap to healing.
- Support this work and help more people.
- Share your triumph and inspire others.

It only takes a moment, but makes a world of difference.

Ready to share your journey? Please scan to Review!

Or visit the following link:

http://amazon.com/review/create-review?&asin=B0F94KKT58

Thank you again. I wish you all the happiness and security in your relationships.

With gratitude,

Eleanor Mercer

REFERENCES

Ainsworth, M., Blehar, D. S., Waters, E., & Wall, S. (1978). *Patterns of attachment: A psychological study of the strange situation.* Psycnet.apa.org. https://psycnet.apa.org/record/1980-50809-000

American Psychiatric Association. (n.d.). *What are anxiety disorders?* https://psychiatry.org/patients-families/anxiety-disorders/what-are-anxiety-disorders#:~:text=Anxiety%20refers%20to%20anticipation%20of

Angelou, M. (n.d.). *Maya Angelou quote.* Goodreads. https://www.goodreads.com/quotes/120991-you-alone-are-enough-you-have-nothing-to-prove-to

Bard, C. (n.d.). *Carl Bard quote.* Tiny Buddha. https://tinybuddha.com/wisdom-quotes/though-no-one-can-go-back-and-make-a-brand-new-start-anyone-can-start-from-now-and-make-a-brand-new-ending/

Batholomew, K., & Horowitz, L. M. (1991). Attachment styles among young adults: A test of a four-category model. *Journal of Personality and*

Social Psychology, 61(2), 226–244.
https://psycnet.apa.org/record/1991-33075-001

Belle, E. (2020, May 22). *Codependency: How emotional neglect turns us into people-pleasers.* Healthline.
https://www.healthline.com/health/mental-health/codependency-and-attachment-trauma

Benoit, D. (2004). Infant-parent attachment: Definition, types, antecedents, measurement and outcome. *Paediatrics & Child Health, 9*(8), 541–545. https://doi.org/10.1093/pch/9.8.541

Benson, H., Greenwood, M. M., & Klemchuk, H. (1975). The relaxation response: Psychophysiologic aspects and clinical applications. *The International Journal of Psychiatry in Medicine, 6*(1-2), 87–98.
https://doi.org/10.2190/376w-e4mt-qm6q-houm

Bowlby, J. (1969). *Attachment and Loss, Vol. 1 Attachment. Attachment and Loss.* New York Basic Books..
https://www.scirp.org/reference/ReferencesPapers?ReferenceID=1162623

Bowlby, J. (n.d.). *John Bowlby quotes.* Goodreads.
https://www.goodreads.com/author/quotes/369172.John_Bowlby

Brandon, D. N. (2022, September 15). *How to improve your anxious attachment style: Tips and strategies.* Dr Nathan Brandon.
https://drnathanbrandon.com/how-to-improve-your-anxious-attachment-style-tips-and-strategies/

Brown, B. (2014). *The gifts of imperfection: Let go of who you think you're supposed to be and embrace who you are.* Instaread Summaries.

Bretherton, I. (1992). The origins of attachment theory: John Bowlby and Mary Ainsworth. Psycnet.apa.org. https://psycnet.apa.org/record/1993-01038-001

Butler, E. A., Egloff, B., Wilhelm, F. H., Smith, N. C., Erickson, E. A., & Gross, J. J. (2003). The social consequences of expressive suppression. *Emotion, 3*(1), 48–67. https://doi.org/10.1037/1528-3542.3.1.48

Cherry, K. (2025, January 29). *What is attachment theory?* Verywell Mind. https://www.verywellmind.com/what-is-attachment-theory-2795337

Choi, J., Marakas, G. M., Singh, S. N., & Lee, K. (2019). Two distinct routes for inducing emotions in HCI design. International Journal of Human-Computer Studies, 124, 67–80. https://doi.org/10.1016/j.ijhcs.2018.11.012

Cohen, G. L., & Sherman, D. K. (2014).The psychology of change: Self-affirmation and social psychological intervention. *Annual Review of Psychology,* 65(1), 333–371. https://doi.org/10.1146/annurev-psych-010213-115137

Collins, N. L., & Read, S. J. (1990). Adult attachment, working models, and relationship quality in dating couples. *Journal of Personality and Social Psychology, 58*(4), 644–663. https://doi.org/10.1037//0022-3514.58.4.644

Copley, L. (2024, July 8). *Anxious attachment style: What it is (+ Its hidden strengths).* PositivePsychology.com. https://positivepsychology.com/anxious-attachment-style/

De Netto, P. M., Quek, K. F., & Golden, K. J. (2021). Communication, the heart of a relationship: examining capitalization, accommodation, and self-construal on relationship satisfaction. *Frontiers in Psychology, 12*(12). https://doi.org/10.3389/fpsyg.2021.767908

Ein-Dor, T., & Hirschberger, G. (2016). Rethinking attachment theory: From a theory of relationships to a theory of individual and group survival. *Current Directions in Psychological Science, 25*(4), 223–227. https://doi.org/10.1177/0963721416650684

Enright, R. D., & Fitzgibbons, R. P. (2000). What forgiveness is not. In R. D. Enright & R. P. Fitzgibbons. *Helping clients forgive: An empirical guide for resolving anger and restoring hope.*, 37–51. American Psychological Association. https://doi.org/10.1037/10381-003

Felman, A. (2022, May 4). *Anxiety treatment: Self-management, therapy, and medication.* Www.medicalnewstoday.com. https://www.medicalnewstoday.com/articles/323494

Gottman, J. (2018, March 22). *How anxious attachment can be healthy in a relationship.* The Gottman Institute. https://www.gottman.com/blog/how-anxious-attachment-can-be-healthy-in-a-relationship/

Gross, J. J. (2002). Emotion regulation: Affective, cognitive, and social consequences. *Psychophysiology, 39*(3), 281–291. https://doi.org/10.1017/s0048577201393198

Hall, J. H., & Fincham, F. D. (2005). Self–forgiveness: The stepchild of forgiveness research. *Journal of Social and Clinical Psychology,* 24(5), 621–637. https://doi.org/10.1521/jscp.2005.24.5.621

Hazan, C., & Shaver, P. R. (2017, November). *Romantic love conceptualized as an attachment process.* ResearchGate. https://www.researchgate.net/publication/345051434_Romantic_Love_Conceptualized_as_an_Attachment_Process

Heller, D. (2019). *The power of attachment: How to create deep and lasting intimate relationships.* Sounds True.

Hendrix, H. (2019). *Harville Hendrix quote.* Goodreads. https://www.goodreads.com/author/quotes/25837.Harville_Hendrix

Hinton, A. O., McReynolds, M. R., Martinez, D., Shuler, H. D., & Termini, C. M. (2020). The power of saying no. *EMBO Reports, 21*(7). https://doi.org/10.15252/embr.202050918

Hoffman, A. A., & Hercus, M. J. (2000). Environmental stress as an evolutionary force. *BioScience, 50*(3), 217. https://doi.org/10.1641/0006-3568(2000)050[0217:esaaef]2.3.co;2

Holland, K. (2018, September 19). *Everything you need to know about anxiety*. Healthline. https://www.healthline.com/health/anxiety

Holmes, J. (2014). *John Bowlby and attachment theory (2nd ed.)*. Apa.org. https://psycnet.apa.org/record/2014-02389-000

Jerath, R., Crawford, M. W., Barnes, V. A., & Harden, K. (2015). Self-regulation of breathing as a primary treatment for anxiety. *Applied Psychophysiology and Biofeedback, 40*(2), 107–115. https://doi.org/10.1007/s10484-015-9279-8

Johnson, S. (2025). *Sue Johnson quote*. Goodreads. https://www.goodreads.com/author/quotes/22726.Sue_Johnson

Johnson, S. M. (2004). Attachment Theory: A Guide for Healing Couple Relationships. In W. S. Rholes & J. A. Simpson (Eds.), *Adult attachment: Theory, research, and clinical implications* (pp. 367–387). Guilford Publications. https://psycnet.apa.org/record/2005-00319-012

Kegan, R. (2009). *Immunity to change : how to overcome it and unlock potential in yourself and your organization*. Harvard Business School, Cop.

Keng, S. L., Smoski, M. J., & Robins, C. J. (2011). Effects of mindfulness on psychological health: A review of empirical studies *Clinical Psychology Review, 31*(6), 1041–1056. https://doi.org/10.1016/j.cpr.2011.04.006

Kernis, M. H. (2003). Toward a conceptualization of optimal self-esteem. *Psychological Inquiry*, 14(1), 1–26. https://doi.org/10.1207/s15327965pli1401_01

Lebow, J. L. (2022). The impact of couple and family interventions. *Family Process*, 61(2), 453–455. https://doi.org/10.1111/famp.12778

LePera, N. (2025). *Nicole LePera quotes*. Goodreads.com. https://www.goodreads.com/work/quotes/75843507-how-to-do-the-work-recognize-your-patterns-heal-from-your-past-and-cr

Levy, K. N., Ellison, W. D., Scott, L. N., & Bernecker, S. L. (2011b). Attachment style. Journal of Clinical Psychology, 67(2), 193–203. https://doi.org/10.1002/jclp.20756

Main, M., & Solomon, J. (1990). Procedures for identifying infants as disorganized/disoriented during the Ainsworth Strange Situation. In M. T. Greenberg, D. Cicchetti, & E. M. Cummings (Eds.), *Attachment in the preschool years: Theory, research, and intervention* (pp. 121–160). The University of Chicago Press. https://psycnet.apa.org/record/1990-98514-004

Mayo Clinic. (2017). *Generalized anxiety disorder - Diagnosis and treatment*. https://www.mayoclinic.org/diseases-conditions/generalized-anxiety-disorder/diagnosis-treatment/drc-20361045

Mayo Clinic. (2018). *Anxiety disorders - symptoms and causes*. https://www.mayoclinic.org/diseases-conditions/anxiety/symptoms-causes/syc-20350961

McLeod, S. (2025, March 20). *John Bowlby's attachment theory.* Simply Psychology. https://www.simplypsychology.org/bowlby.htm l

McMurtrie, R. J. (2022). Observing, recording, visualising and interpreting visitors' movement patterns in art museums: A mixed method approach. *Multimodality & Society, 2*(2), 93–113. https://doi.org/10.1177/26349795221100132

Mikulincer, M., & Shaver, P. R. (2007). *Attachment in adulthood: Structure, dynamics, and change.* Guilford Press. https://psycnet.apa.org/record/2007-12400-000

Mikulincer, M., & Shaver, P. R. (2010). Attachment in Adulthood, First Edition: Structure, Dynamics, and Change. In *Google Books.* Guilford Publications. https://books.google.ca/books?hl=en&lr=&id=5 egODAAAQBAJ&oi=fnd&pg=PR1&dq=Mikulinc er

Mikulincer, M., & Shaver, P. R. (2016, January). *Adult attachment strategies and the regulation of emotion.* ResearchGate; unknown. https://www.researchgate.net/publication/309 905037_Adult_attachment_strategies_and_the _regulation_of_emotion

Mohammadkhani, S., Bahari, A., & Akbarian FiroozAbadi, M. (2017). Attachment styles and depression symptoms: The mediating role of rumination. *Iranian Journal of Psychiatry and Clinical Psychology, 23*(3), 320–335. https://doi.org/10.29252/nirp.ijpcp.23.3.320

Molina, G. (2024, June 3). *Managing instant gratification: A therapist's guide.* Fitcy Health. https://fitcyhealth.com/advice/instant-gratification/

Naor, L., & Mayseless, O. (2020). The art of working with nature in nature-based therapies. *Journal of Experiential Education, 44*(2), 184-202. https://doi.org/10.1177/1053825920933639

National Institutes of Health. (n.d.). A*nxiety disorders.* https://www.hhs.gov/answers/mental-health-and-substance-abuse/what-are-the-five-major-types-of-anxiety-disorders/index.html

Neff, K. (2003). The development and validation of a scale to measure self-compassion. *Self and Identity, 2*(3), 223–250. https://doi.org/10.1080/15298860309027

Neff, K. (2023, September 23). *Kristen Neff Quotes.* Ineffable Living. https://ineffableliving.com/best-self-compassion-quotes/

Newman, M. G., Castonguay, L. G., Jacobson, N. C., & Moore, G. A. (2015). Adult attachment as a moderator of treatment outcome for generalized anxiety disorder: Comparison between cognitive–behavioral therapy (CBT) plus supportive listening and CBT plus interpersonal and emotional processing therapy. *Journal of Consulting and Clinical Psychology, 83*(5), 915–925. https://doi.org/10.1037/a0039359

Peel, R., & Caltabiano, N. (2020). Why do we sabotage love? A thematic analysis of lived experiences of relationship breakdown and maintenance. *Journal of Couple & Relationship Therapy, 20*(2), 1–33. https://doi.org/10.1080/15332691.2020.179503 9

Pressman, S. D., Matthews, K. A., Cohen, S., Martire, L. M., Scheier, M., Baum, A., & Schulz, R. (2009). Association of enjoyable leisure activities with psychological and physical well-being. *Psychosomatic Medicine, 71*(7), 725–732. https://doi.org/10.1097/psy.0b013e3181ad7978

Rogers, C. (1961b). *On becoming a person: A therapist's view of psychotherapy.* Houghton Mifflin. https://teots.org/wp-content/uploads/2021/08/On-becoming-a-person-by-Rogers-Carl-R.-z-lib.org_.pdf

Rogers, C. (2019). *Carl Rogers quote.* Goodreads. https://www.goodreads.com/quotes/50836-the-curious-paradox-is-that-when-i-accept-myself-just

Rosenberg, M. (2012). *Marshall B. Rosenberg quote.* Goodreads. https://www.goodreads.com/author/quotes/40 541.Marshall_B_Rosenberg

Ryan, R. M., & Deci, E. L. (2000). *Self-determination Theory and the Facilitation of Intrinsic motivation, Social development, and well-being.* Psycnet.apa.org. https://psycnet.apa.org/doiLanding?doi=10.103 7%2F0003-066X.55.1.68

Simpson, J. A., & Rholes, W. S. (2017). Adult attachment, stress, and romantic relationships. *Current Opinion in Psychology*, *13*(13), 19–24. https://doi.org/10.1016/j.copsyc.2016.04.006

Smith, A. L. (2024, November 28). *Social media on attachment and relationships*. Adam Lane Smith. https://adamlanesmith.com/social-media-on-attachment/

Strand, P. S., Vossen, J. J., & Savage, E. (2019). Culture and Child Attachment Patterns: a Behavioral Systems Synthesis. *Perspectives on Behavior Science*, *42*(4), 835–850. https://doi.org/10.1007/s40614-019-00220-3

Tatkin, S. (2011). *Wired for love: How understanding your partner's brain and attachment style can help you defuse conflict and build a secure relationship*. New Harbinger Publications.

Tatkin, S. (2025). Stan Tatkin quotes. Goodreads.com. https://www.goodreads.com/author/quotes/3257055.Stan_Tatkin

White, M., & Epston, D. (1990). *Narrative means to therapeutic ends*. Norton.

Witvliet, C. van O., Ludwig, T. E., & Laan, K. L. V. (2001). Granting Forgiveness or Harboring Grudges: Implications for Emotion, Physiology, and Health. Psychological Science, 12(2), 117–123. https://doi.org/10.1111/1467-9280.00320

www.ingramcontent.com/pod-product-compliance
Lightning Source LLC
Chambersburg PA
CBHW031153020426
42333CB00013B/638